WESTERN & CENTRAL OREGON

WESTERN
& CENTRAL
OREGON

SECOND EDITION

BONNIE HENDERSON

THE
MOUNTAINEERS

Published by
The Mountaineers
1001 SW Klickitat Way, Suite 201
Seattle, WA 98134

First edition, 1992, Second edition, 1999

Published simultaneously in Great Britain by Cordee, 3a DeMontfort Street, Leicester, England, LE1 7HD

Manufactured in Canada

Edited by Karen Parkin
Maps by Pease Press
All photographs by Bonnie Henderson, except for the following: Michael S. Thompson, pages 143, 145, 168, 251; Paul D. Hoobyar, pages 111, 146.
Cover design and book design by Jennifer LaRock Shontz
Layout by Jacqulyn Weber

Cover photograph: *Picnickers in paintbrush enjoy misty view of Oregon Coast Range and Willamette Valley from Mary's Peak summit*
© Michael S. Thompson
Frontispiece: *North and Middle Sister, from Little Belknap Crater Trail*

Library of Congress Cataloging-in-Publication Data
Henderson, Bonnie.
    Best hikes with children in western & central Oregon / Bonnie Henderson. — 2nd ed.
        p. cm.
    ISBN 0-89886-575-1 (pbk.)
    1. Hiking—Oregon Guidebooks. 2. Family recreation—Oregon Guidebooks. 3. Oregon Guidebooks. I. Title.
    GV199.42.O7 H46 1999
    917.9504'43—dc21
                                                                99-6650
                                                                   CIP

CONTENTS

SOUTHERN CASCADES AND SISKIYOUS

EAST OF THE CASCADES

THE COAST

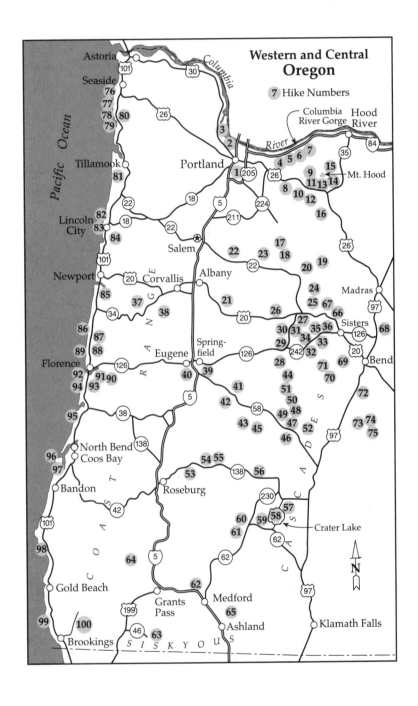

Western and Central Oregon

7 Hike Numbers

Columbia River Gorge
Hood River

ACKNOWLEDGMENTS

Thanks to all the national forest and state parks personnel who offered advice on trails, based on both their professional knowledge and their personal experience with their own children.

Thanks to all the friends who accompanied me on hikes—or didn't, but who stayed in touch, stayed supportive, through a very busy year of writing and hiking.

Thanks to the many friends and colleagues at PeaceHealth who have offered feedback and encouragement over the years.

Thanks to my incredibly supportive family, writers all, and especially my dad, who nurtured a love of woods and walking.

A NOTE ABOUT SAFETY

Safety is an important concern in all outdoor activities. No guidebook can alert you to every hazard or anticipate the limitations of every reader. Therefore, the descriptions of roads, trails, routes, and natural features in this book are not representations that a particular place or excursion will be safe for your party. When you follow any of the routes described in this book, you assume responsibility for your own safety. Under normal conditions, such excursions require the usual attention to traffic, road and trail conditions, weather, terrain, the capabilities of your party, and other factors. Keeping informed on current conditions and exercising common sense are the keys to a safe, enjoyable outing.

The Mountaineers

KEY TO SYMBOLS

 Easy trails. These are relatively short, level, gentle trails suitable for small children or first-time hikers. Hiking boots are often unnecessary, except to keep feet dry.

 Moderate trails. Most of these are at least 3 miles round-trip distance and/or have an elevation gain of more than 500 feet. The trail may be rough and uneven in places.

 Strenuous trails. These trails are generally at least 5 miles round-trip distance and/or involve considerable elevation gain. The route may be rough and uneven. These trails are suitable for older or experienced children.

 Hikable. The best times of year to hike each trail are indicated by the following symbols: flower—spring; sun—summer; leaf—fall; snowflake—winter.

 Driving directions. These paragraphs tell you how to get to the trailheads.

 Turnarounds. These are places where families can cut a hike short yet still have a satisfying outing. Turnarounds usually offer picnic opportunities, views, or special natural attractions.

 Cautions. These mark potential hazards—cliffs, stream crossings, and the like—where close supervision of children is strongly recommended.

 Day hikes. These hikes can easily be completed in a day or part of a day. Camping along the trail is not recommended or is prohibited.

 Backpack trips. Overnight camping is permitted along the trail in designated areas (some with structures or facilities), or a public campground is within reasonable walking distance of the hiking trail. In every case, the campground or camping area appears on the accompanying map.

INTRODUCTION

WHY HIKE WITH CHILDREN?

Some kids take to hiking like fish to water. There's our nine-year-old friend John Mbuki, who with his mom, Diane, has field-tested at least half of the hikes in the first edition, and nine-year-old Zoë, who thinks my job—going hiking and then writing about it—would be about the best job in the world. Max, age ten, doesn't usually like the *idea* of hiking but he always winds up enjoying himself, especially when he can bring his dog, Sadie.

But for others—among them, frankly, my own son—getting them out hiking can be a struggle. Reluctant young hikers will do their best to discourage you. Add to their whining the gear gathering, the arrangements required to bring friends along, the driving, the logistics, and it's easy to get discouraged.

Why bother? For the same reason that we feed them not just junk food but healthy food: because they require it to grow, to thrive, perhaps even to survive. "Children need contact with the natural world," writes Mary Pipher, author of *Reviving Ophelia* and *The Shelter of Each Other*. "It's an antidote to advertising and gives them a different perspective on the universe. Looking at the Milky Way makes most of us feel small and yet a part of something vast. Television, with its emphasis on meeting every need, makes people feel self-important and yet unconnected to anything greater than themselves."

Pipher's thoughts are echoed by evolutionary biologist Edward Wilson, who hypothesizes that human beings have a deep, genetically based need to connect with the rest of the natural world. Meeting this need, he says, may be as important to human health as forming close, personal relationships. And nearly two generations ago—before TV, before video games—scientist Rachel Carson drew similar conclusions in an article she published for parents entitled, "Help Your Child to Wonder":

"What is the value of preserving and strengthening this sense of awe and wonder, this recognition of something beyond the boundaries of human existence? Is the exploration of the natural world just a pleasant way to pass the golden hours of childhood, or is there something deeper?

Benson Lake

"I am sure there is something much deeper, something lasting and significant. Those who dwell, as scientists or laymen, among the beauties and mysteries of the earth are never alone or weary of life....Those who contemplate the beauty of the earth find reserves of strength that will endure as long as life lasts."

So we continue on, loading the car with our kids and their friends, luring them with snacks, packing and unpacking packs and cars. Because it's as necessary to children as calcium and Vitamin C, as air. Not necessarily every weekend. But necessarily now and again.

I was lucky that my growing-up years were filled with trips into the wilderness. But looking back now, I place these adventures into two categories: tedious, goal-oriented hikes, or fun, exploratory hikes. The first category includes a slog up a steep scree slope on a blazing summer day and portions of a backpack trip in Idaho that I remember as too long and, again, too hot. The second category was pure magic: wandering awestruck in a cathedral-like old-growth forest, fording creeks on fallen logs and pursuing orange-bellied salamanders across the mossy forest floor, backpacking into a hidden lake so full of trout we could pick the fish we'd have for dinner before we cast.

I hope this book helps you create more family outings that fall into that second category. The following approaches have helped other adults create memorable outings for kids. Try them on yours.

Remember that not all three-year-olds fit size three pajamas. A child's readiness for hiking is just as variable. Your kids will let you know when they're ready for a new challenge.

No siblings? "Adopt" some. The extra hassle of taking more children on a hike is generally outweighed by the greater level of cooperation and plain fun your child is likely to have with a friend or two along.

Assign an *engine* and *caboose* and rotate these roles. The child in front, setting the pace, enjoys the perks—and a taste of the responsibility—that come with leadership. The caboose has the important job of ensuring that no one falls far behind (and, in the process, can feel as important as the engine).

Take plenty of snacks—even for a half-hour outing. Children need the energy boost, and snacks—carefully rationed—can help keep enthusiasm high.

Be generous with praise. It can do more to raise energy levels than all the granola bars in the world.

Balance new hikes with old favorites. Children often enjoy returning to favorite spots; vary the experience by going in different seasons or at different times of day. Choose trails with special attractions scattered at intervals; as your children grow, so may the distances they're willing and able to hike.

Be a tortoise, not always a hare. Slowly, with a lot of stops to catch grasshoppers or poke under rocks, your tortoises will usually get there. They may balk if required to travel at your adult hare's pace.

Encourage a family wilderness ethic. By pointing out indiscretions of other hikers—an empty pop can beside the trail, shortcuts worn between switchbacks—and explaining why your family doesn't do that, you enlist your children as conservationists before it occurs to them to cut across those switchbacks themselves.

Don't confuse family hikes with adult workouts. Reaching target heart rate has little allure for children. When you're out with the kids, be willing to take it slow. Try getting in your workout, if it's important to you, before a family hike so you're not rushed and frustrated.

Remember your real goal. Do you want to reach the summit of a particular mountain, or to nurture your children's curiosity and sense of adventure and instill a love of the outdoors that will last a lifetime? The patience you demonstrate while the kids tarry over a mysterious hole in the ground, or while they stop—again—to rest and snack will reward you many times over.

HOW TO USE THIS BOOK

Anything can spoil a hike, especially for youngsters new to the outdoors whose tolerance for cold, heat, fatigue, bugs, and even long car rides can be limited at best. A parent's first job is to choose trails carefully. I selected the hikes in this book for their appeal to kids *and* for their relative ease—children may go farther on a difficult, but interesting, trail than on a flat, but boring, trail. Most of the trails lie close to main roads and don't require a tedious drive on gravel logging roads. They were also chosen with an eye toward geographical balance. Hence, many excellent trails were omitted. This book offers only a selection of the most interesting, relatively short trails in western and central Oregon; it is in no way a definitive list.

Most of the trails included here go no farther than 1.5 miles without a treat of some kind: a waterfall, a bridge, a lake, a great view, a mountain of glass, or a tunnel of lava. That way, if hikers go no farther than this turnaround point, everyone can still come away with a sense of accomplishment. This guide steers away from view hikes that require a long uphill slog before offering any reward. By the time your child is ready to switchback 4 miles up a relatively uninteresting trail to reach a stellar viewpoint, you no longer need this book.

Hikes are grouped geographically, oriented to major population centers (or, in the case of the coast, natural geographic boundaries). Some hikes stand by themselves, but in most cases several hikes are clustered around a major highway, giving car campers several choices for day trips during a family vacation.

Selecting a Hike

Glance at the capsule descriptions at the beginning of each hike in the area you intend to visit. These provide a snapshot of the hike—once you know how to read them.

Type: All the hikes in this book are short enough to be enjoyed as day hikes, meaning one-day or partial-day outings. If a hike is listed as a day hike only (not "day hike or backpack"), that means that overnighting is impractical (due to rough terrain, lack of water, etc.), inadvisable (due to a delicate environment), or prohibited.

Difficulty: The designation of a trail as easy, moderate, or strenuous for children takes into consideration the trail condition, elevation gain, and distance to the major destination. Often children can travel long distances on level trails, especially with interesting distractions along the way. Add some elevation gain and long stretches without much variation in scenery, and the fatigue level quickly goes

Beach at Devils Elbow, below Heceta Head

up. If a short hike is what you're after, don't limit your choices to those designated "easy"; even a trail rated "strenuous" may in fact be easy and full of interest for the first mile, making that section a good choice for beginning hikers. Add your own judgment to the formula as well; an exposed ridgeline trail that's a breeze on a balmy June day can quickly turn into a nightmare in blistering heat or persistent rain, especially with very young, tired, or inexperienced hikers.

Distance: For each hike, the total mileage for the outing is listed. A round-trip hike is the total distance to the destination and back out. A loop hike's mileage includes the loop distance and any walking necessary to reach the start of the loop. One-way hikes are those with trailheads accessible by car at either end. With a shuttle car, you can make these one-way hikes in one direction only (most appealing when the hike is downhill); if you intend to walk from one end to the other and back without the shuttle car, hike mileage will double.

Hikable: This line generally indicates the months the trail is snow-free in a typical year, though the actual hiking season will vary from year to year according to snowpack and weather conditions. In some cases road closures dictate the hike's seasonal accessibility.

High point: This number indicates the height above sea level of the highest point on the trail section described. Use it as a clue to how cold or exposed the trail might be, or how early or late in the year it might open up.

Terrain: A brief description is given for each hike's terrain, from level or nearly so, to steep ascents. Any significant elevation gain required on a round-trip hike is approximated in feet.

WHAT TO TAKE

"My own pack!"

Particularly with younger children, offering a pack of their own to carry can add excitement to an outing. You don't have to put much in it—the less the better, at first—but you may find you get more cooperation from a child wearing a pack. It seems to signal that you consider the wearer a bona fide member of the party, not just a youngster the adults brought along on their outing.

Small packs sized for children are widely available, but a smallish adult's day pack may get used for more years; just don't overload it. Children also love fanny packs. One woman I know adds something special to her grandchild's pack every time they hike: colorful adhesive bandages, a small flashlight, and an emergency whistle.

Boots or shoes?

Athletic shoes are fine on dry, level trails. But flat soles offer no help with traction. Buy boots if you plan to do any significant hiking with your child.

All-leather hiking boots for children may be too stiff, especially for the very young. Look for pliable, split-grain leather boots with a soft collar and treat them for water-repellency (or you'll lose one of their primary advantages: keeping feet dry). Combination leather and fabric boots tend to be lighter, though not quite as water-repellent. Stiffer boots may require a breaking-in period; have children wear them around the house at first to make sure they fit, then around the neighborhood before embarking on a major outing. Then, just in case, carry moleskin and apply it at the *first* sign of discomfort.

The Ten Essentials

You say you're planning to hike only 2 miles, and the weather's beautiful? It's still a good idea to make sure most, if not all, of the following items are in your day pack, especially when hiking with children. This list, compiled by The Mountaineers, has become an accepted standard for hikers and other recreationists.

1. **Extra clothing.** Not necessarily a complete set of clothes, but do take at least one more sweater than you think you'll need and, on all but the best summer days, rain gear. Extra socks are a good idea. Take lightweight water shoes if you plan to do much wading.
2. **Extra food.** Pack what you plan to eat—and then some, just in case. The traditional hiker's menu consists of high-energy,

noncrushable foods that won't spoil too quickly, such as dried fruits, nuts, hard crackers, cheese and dried meats, and—in limited quantity—candy. Fresh fruit is heavier but refreshing. Pick foods your children don't ordinarily get, or save certain treats for outings (dried fruit rolls or boxed juices, for example), to make hikes special.

3. **Sunglasses.** Children of hiking age usually like to wear shades, especially if they've helped to pick them out. Encouraging kids to wear sunglasses now (especially if they're around water and snow) helps reduce their chances of developing cataracts years down the road.

4. **Knife.** One with various blades and gadgets is particularly useful (for adults, and eventually for whittling kids).

5. **Fire starter.** A candle or chemical fire starter of some kind adds little weight to the pack and can be a lifesaver if you wind up bivouacking unexpectedly.

6. **First-aid kit.** Keep it supplied with the basics, plus any special medications your group requires such as a bee sting kit if someone is allergic.

7. **Matches.** Waterproof matches, available at sporting goods stores, are the safest; in any case, keep them in a secure, waterproof container. An inexpensive lighter or two are also handy to keep in a pack.

8. **Flashlight.** Tiny, light, but powerful minilights are widely available.

9. **Map.** Many of the trails in this book aren't so isolated or complicated that they require a map for route-finding, though it's always a good idea to carry one. Older children may enjoy learning to read maps in the field. Maps are often necessary for finding your way on the sometimes complicated network of roads leading to national forest trailheads.

10. **Compass.** Useless unless you've learned how to use it with a map.

. . . And Then Some

Mosquito repellent. Nothing can spoil a hike in the woods faster than a swarm of mosquitoes. They're annoying enough for adults; they'll quickly ruin a hike for kids. The best defense is a chemical repellent of some kind. "Natural" repellents with ingredients such as citronella sometimes work, though they may require frequent reapplication to be of any use. Otherwise virtually all repellents use the chemical *N, N-diethyl-m-toluamide*, nicknamed DEET, as the active ingredient, in concentrations as high as 95 percent. Avoid the higher concentrations, for at least three reasons. They've been linked to serious health problems and are especially not advised for young children. They can actually melt paint or smear the color in vinyl car seats. And they're not much more effective than the low-end concentrations of about 6.5 percent, though you may have to reapply these more frequently. Wearing a long-sleeved shirt and long pants helps as well.

Water. It's unfortunate, but true: There's really no place in the wilderness where the water is considered safe from giardia. This protozoan, carried by human and animal feces, can cause severe diarrhea of a type that can be hard to diagnose (but easy to treat once it is diagnosed). For short day hikes, drink only water out of water bottles filled at reliable sources—a home tap or a faucet at the trailhead. On longer outings, the simplest defense is to carry a portable water filter. Filters vary in cost and weight, but there are lightweight, reasonably priced models that can filter out giardia and other impurities. Alternatives include boiling water for 20 minutes (using up precious fuel) or treating water with iodine or other chemicals available at hiking stores.

Marion Lake

Toilet paper. The first Murphy's Law of Hiking with Children: Regardless of how many potty stops you make beforehand, someone has to "go to the bathroom" within 20 minutes of leaving the last bathroom. I like to carry two plastic self-sealing bags, one for dry toilet paper and the other for used TP. You can bury the used toilet paper, but it could get dug up and scattered by animals. Some people burn their used toilet paper. I suggest treating it like any other litter and packing it out. Be sure to bury feces at least 6 inches deep, far from the trail or water sources. Use a stick to dig or, better yet, carry a lightweight plastic trowel.

Sunscreen. Dermatologists now warn that sunburn on young children can be a precursor to skin cancer years later; conversely, protecting children from sunburn in their early years does a lot to help them stay healthy as adults. Some children are allergic to PABA, the active ingredient in most sunscreens; pediatricians suggest using a non-PABA lotion with a sun protection factor (SPF) of at least fifteen to thirty if skin is very fair or, with adults, there's a history of skin cancer or precancerous lesions.

SAFETY

It's easy to be lulled into complacency by a sunny day, a good trail, and your own physical strength and feeling of competence. But as anyone with any experience knows, the wilderness can be a dangerous place for the unprepared; conditions can change quickly, and accidents do sometimes happen. You can reduce your chances of disaster by covering two bases. First, be prepared. Learn something about the area you'll be going into and carry adequate emergency supplies. In classes or on the trail with more experienced companions, learn survival skills, including how to use a map and compass. Second, know your own limits and those of your party, and respect them.

All the trails in this guide have been field-checked, but conditions and routes change. The trail ratings (easy, moderate, and strenuous) are estimations: Use them as guidelines, not as fact. Use your own best judgment to keep your party safe.

HYPOTHERMIA AND HEAT EXHAUSTION

When they're excited and having fun, children can go a long time before they realize they've overdone it. In cold, wet weather, as in baking heat, it's imperative that adults keep a sharp eye on children to look for signs of these two ailments and attend to preventive measures before more serious symptoms appear.

Summit of Spencer Butte

Hypothermia is a potentially life-threatening drop in core body temperature that most often occurs in cold, wet weather but can occur any time: on a windy spring day, for example, when you stop for lunch and don't bother putting a sweater on your sweat-cooled body. To help prevent hypothermia, wear clothing in layers—wool and polypropylene rather than all cotton—and peel them off or pile them back on as your body temperature fluctuates. Always carry (and wear, when necessary) good rain gear. If someone in your party starts shivering; seems disoriented; has cold, clammy skin; or simply seems listless and whiny, get him moving, get clothes on him, and get hot liquids into him as quickly as possible. On cooler days it's nice to carry a thermos of hot chocolate or cider—or have one waiting back in the car.

Heat exhaustion is as easy to get as it is to prevent. You get it by not taking in as much liquid as you are eliminating, and you prevent it by drinking more water than you may think you need. Most children can't be depended upon to drink as much water as they need on very hot days; it's the adults' responsibility to suggest water stops more often than children think necessary. Give a child her own special water bottle and she's more likely to drink up.

The symptoms of heat exhaustion are deceptively like flu; I've been out with kids who insisted that they had the flu but whose symptoms subsided in a matter of minutes once they got treatment for heat exhaustion. Don't expect hot skin; people with heat exhaustion usually have a normal or slightly depressed temperature. If anyone in your party is feeling faint, nauseated, or dizzy and feels his heart beating rapidly—especially if the weather's hot and you suspect he hasn't been drinking enough water—get him to lie down in a cool, comfortable place and start sipping, then drinking, fluids—salty fluids if you have them, but anything will help. You should notice rapid improvement.

GOOD TRAIL MANNERS

Most of these are obvious, but just for review:

Don't litter. Better yet, bring an extra plastic bag to bring out others' trash you might find.

Don't pick anything. Leave the flowers—and for that matter, the colorful mushrooms and the hermit crabs—to live out their natural lives and to let others enjoy seeing them.

Stay on the trail, rather than cutting across switchbacks, which leads to erosion.

Don't camp on lakeshores or in other delicate environments.

Keep dogs on leash if there are other hikers around. It's required in wilderness areas and on certain other trails. Where dogs are prohibited, that's mentioned in the initial hike description.

TRAILHEAD FEES

As this book goes to press, the U.S. Forest Service is in the third year of a demonstration project charging three dollars or more to park at many trailheads in Northwest national forests, including within Oregon Dunes National Recreation Area on the central coast. Other managing agencies have jumped on the trailhead fee bandwagon as well (or were already on it): Oregon State Parks, Crater Lake National Park (ten dollars per car in 1999), Sauvie Island

Wildlife Area, and the Bureau of Land Management. At this point you should probably count on paying a fee wherever you go. Fee collection booths and self-pay stations are set up at state parks and at some Forest Service trailheads. Otherwise, you can purchase in advance one-day and annual passes at state park and national forest offices.

SUGGESTIONS?

I've hiked and, in some cases, rehiked all the trails in this book and checked road names and numbers and directions. But changes do occur; trails fall into disrepair; new roads are built or road numbers and names are changed; and old, abandoned trails are rehabilitated. I would appreciate hearing from readers about discrepancies in the hike descriptions and receiving suggestions of other trails that might deserve inclusion in the next edition of *Best Hikes for Children in Western and Central Oregon*. Please write to me in care of The Mountaineers Books, 1001 SW Klickitat Way, Suite 201, Seattle, WA 98134.

KEY TO MAP SYMBOLS

⑤	Interstate	——	Paved Road	△	Summit
㉖	US Highway	– – –	Gravel Road	■	Building
㉒	State Highway	- - - - -	Trail	●	Point of Interest
46	Forest Road	▬▬▬	Boardwalk	○	Town or City
Ⓛ	Lookout	⌒	River or Creek	⊐	Bridge
Ⓣ	Trailhead	—⊩—	Falls	▲	Campground
▬	Parking Lot or Pullout	⸺	Marsh	⛾	Picnic Area
		▬▬	Wilderness or Park Boundary	⛵	Boat Launch

Umbrella Falls, East Fork Hood River

PORTLAND, THE COLUMBIA GORGE, AND MOUNT HOOD

1 TRYON CREEK

Type ▪ Day hike
Hikable ▪ Year-round
Contact ▪ Tryon Creek State Park, (503) 636-9886

CEDAR TRAIL LOOP
Difficulty ▪ Easy for children
Distance ▪ 2.3 miles, loop
Terrain ▪ Rolling (125 feet elevation gain)
High point ▪ 250 feet

LEWIS AND CLARK TRAIL LOOP
Difficulty ▪ Easy for children
Distance ▪ 1.75 miles, loop
Terrain ▪ Rolling (125 feet elevation gain)
High point ▪ 120 feet

Portlanders are fortunate to have a variety of woodsy hiking trails—not just interpretive paths, not just in manicured parks—in and just beyond the city limits. Tryon Creek State Park is a stellar example. Surrounded by suburban southwest Portland, the park's 635 acres are forested in Douglas fir, big-leaf maple, alder, and western red cedar. Footbridges of all description cross Tryon and its feeder creeks. The outstanding trillium bloom here peaks in late March most years.

Hikers can create loops of any length on the park's intricate network of hiking trails (8 miles) and horse trails (3.5 miles, hikers allowed, few horses). Trails are extremely well signed. Come prepared for mud in winter. Here are just two of many options for loop hikes in the park.

From I-5 in southwest Portland, take exit 297 and follow Southwest Terwilliger Boulevard south 2.8 miles to the park entrance on the right. Begin hiking at the park's Nature Center, which has park information and maps, interpretive exhibits, and a gift shop.

CEDAR TRAIL LOOP

From the Nature Center, walk south on Old Main Trail 0.25 mile, passing Big Fir Trail, then bear left on Red Fox Trail to drop down to Tryon Creek at Red Fox Bridge. Cross the bridge, go another 0.1 mile, and bear right onto Cedar Trail. Follow it 1.2 miles—past

Hemlock Trail, over Bunk Bridge, all the way to High Bridge. Across the bridge, make a sharp right onto Middle Creek Trail, then bear left on Maple Ridge Trail to return to the Nature Center.

LEWIS AND CLARK TRAIL LOOP

This trail reportedly has the best show of trilliums in early spring and includes a trip across a bouncy suspension footbridge. From the

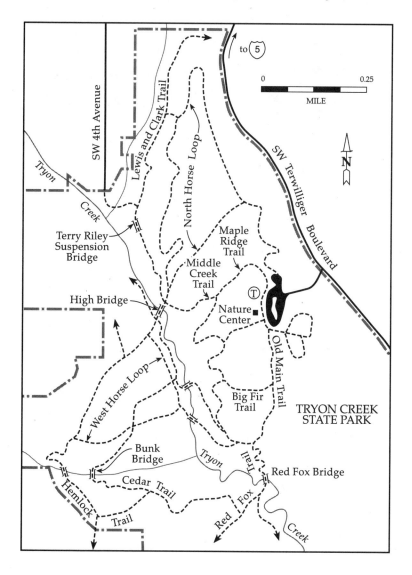

Side creek footbridge, Tryon Creek State Park

Nature Center, head north on Maple Ridge and Middle Creek Trails 0.4 mile to High Bridge. Don't cross; continue straight on the trail closest to the creek. In about 0.25 mile you'll reach Terry Riley Suspension Bridge spanning a gully. Bear right at the end of the bridge to get on Lewis and Clark Trail; keep your eyes open for the delicate white or pink flower. About 0.4 mile from the bridge, turn right, then a quick left to take North Horse Loop 0.8 mile to the equestrian area just north of the Nature Center.

2 OAK ISLAND

Type	Day hike
Difficulty	Easy for children
Distance	3 miles, loop
Terrain	Nearly level
High point	20 feet
Hikable	Mid-April through September
Contact	Sauvie Island Wildlife Area, (503) 621-3488

Sauvie Island lies at the meeting of the Willamette and Columbia Rivers, northwest of Portland—a pastoral island of farms and fields,

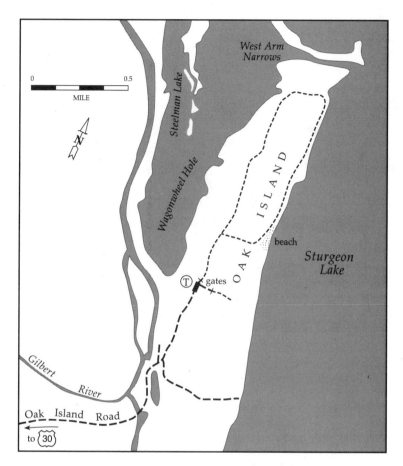

much of it protected by the state as a wildlife refuge. At the heart of Sauvie Island lies Sturgeon Lake, and jutting into the lake is a peninsula of tall oaks and open fields. An "island" on an island: remote, breezy. There are views—sparkling lake through blackberry thicket—but it's the variety of sounds that strikes you here: the mixed chorus of birds, the wind in the oaks, now and then a jet approaching the Portland airport. The trail is closed to hikers during hunting season, formerly into February, but a new goose restoration project lengthened the closure to mid-April in 1999.

From downtown Portland take US Highway 30 about 10 miles to the Sauvie Island Bridge; cross it and head north on Sauvie Island Road. After 1.8 miles, turn right on Reeder Road, go 1.3 miles, and then turn left onto Oak Island Road. Continue 4 miles up and over the dike to the trailhead and gate at road's end.

Sturgeon Lake from Oak Island

From the gate, walk straight down the old road 0.3 mile to where the trail splits. For a clockwise hike, bear left onto the trail threading between oak forest and broad field, with the lake beyond. After rounding the end of the peninsula the trail runs closer to shore with good views of the lake, much wider on this side. At 2.25 miles, at a little pebble beach, a small hiker sign urges you to the right, back through the oak grove at the heart of the peninsula to the start of the loop. Follow the main trail back to your car.

3 VIRGINIA LAKE

Type ▪	Day hike
Difficulty ▪	Easy for children
Distance ▪	2.2 miles, loop
Terrain ▪	Nearly level
High point ▪	40 feet
Hikable ▪	Year-round
Contact ▪	Sauvie Island Wildlife Area, (503) 621-3488

The trail around Virginia Lake is a quiet beauty all year long. You may see birds on the lake; a blind helps you hide while you watch.

You will see boats on the river where the trail cuts back toward Multnomah Channel. Bring a picnic; in a pinch, you can huddle under the covered shelter near the start of the trail.

From downtown Portland take US Highway 30 about 10 miles to the Sauvie Island Bridge; cross it and head north on Sauvie Island Road 2.5 miles. The trailhead is signed "Wapato Access Greenway"; here there is parking for perhaps ten cars.

Walk around the gate and down the trail heading out from the parking area. At 0.2 mile you'll reach a rise to the covered picnic shelter. For a clockwise hike, bear left, past the shelter, and drop down toward the lake, passing a spur trail leading directly to the lake (or, in summer, the marsh). About 0.3 mile from the start of the loop you'll reach a wooden bird blind. Cross the end of the lake and bear right at the junction, or detour left a short distance to Hadley's Landing, where boaters can tie up and hikers can sight-see or picnic with a water view. Continuing on the loop, the trail veers away from the lake's edge, following close to Multnomah Channel with frequent views of the water. Emerging from the trees, the trail crosses the north end of the lake at 1.2 miles and ascends a short rise, offering views of neighboring farms. The trail returns you to the picnic shelter at 1.8 miles; return to the trailhead as you came.

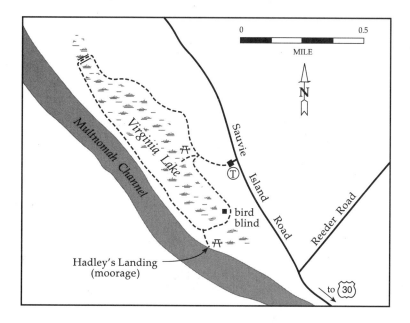

Virginia Lake

 # LATOURELL FALLS

Type ▪	Day hike
Difficulty ▪	Easy to moderate for children
Distance ▪	1 to 2.2 miles, loop
Terrain ▪	Steady ascent (270 to 550 feet elevation gain)
High point ▪	700 feet
Hikable ▪	Most of the year
Contact ▪	Columbia River Gorge National Scenic Area, (541) 386-2333

As magical as most waterfall-blessed gorge trails are, this one seems even more like a path through a fairyland, especially in early spring, with butterflies dancing above pink bleeding hearts and white trilliums blooming on the lush, green hillsides. Little footbridges and a huge natural amphitheater make the gorge at the falls' base particularly

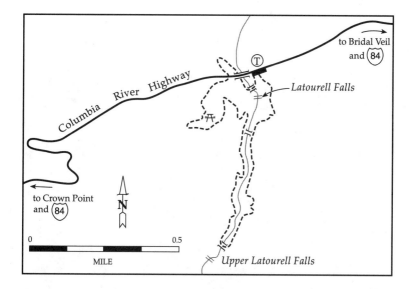

impressive. The trail is formed like a figure eight; for a shorter hike, follow just the lower loop. Hike the lower loop clockwise to save the best for last.

From Portland take I-84 east to exit 28 (Bridal Veil) and backtrack west on the old Columbia River Highway 3 miles to the parking area and overlook at the base of 249-foot Latourell Falls. Left of the falls, an asphalt path leads up the hill a short distance to a viewpoint. From here, the trail turns to dirt, leading to a second overlook near the top of the falls.

Drop down (passing under a quirky tree overhanging the trail) to a footbridge not far above the falls. Stand on the bridge and close your eyes, not only to hear but also to feel the rumbling falls in your feet. If your party is game, backtrack a few steps to a trail junction, turn right, and follow the trail up along the east side of the creek about 0.5 mile to the footbridge at the base of Upper Latourell Falls. The trail continues down the west side of the creek to meet the lower trail just west of the lower falls footbridge.

From here, the trail drops down to the highway at a picnic area 0.2 mile west of the parking area. Rather than return on the road, cross it, drop down some steps and a couple of switchbacks, then bear right, following an asphalt path under the highway and over a footbridge at the base of the falls. Linger a while in this magnificent basalt amphitheater before continuing up to the parking area.

Latourell Falls

5 HORSETAIL FALLS–ONEONTA FALLS

Type	▪ Day hike
Difficulty	▪ Easy for children
Distance	▪ 2.75 miles, loop
Terrain	▪ Rolling, or steady ascent (500 feet elevation gain)
High point	▪ 400 feet
Hikable	▪ Most of the year
Contact	▪ Columbia River Gorge National Scenic Area, (541)386-2333

This trail starts at a waterfall and heads up, offering something you don't get on every hike: the chance to walk behind a falls. The trail also leads you above and below Oneonta Gorge, a gorgeous chasm. Enjoy wildflowers in spring, brilliant big-leaf maple in fall, and lush ferns in every season. Note that the loop hike ends with 0.5 mile along the road shoulder; take only children who will use appropriate caution here (or who are small enough to carry).

From Portland take I-84 east to exit 35 and swing around to head west 1.5 miles on the old Columbia River Highway. (Heading east on the old highway, go 1.5 miles past Multnomah Falls.) Park in the lot across from 176-foot Horsetail Falls, a narrow cataract.

From the signed trailhead left of the falls, head uphill toward Upper Horsetail Falls (also called Ponytail Falls), passing through a garden of maidenhair and other ferns. At 0.25 mile turn west onto Columbia Gorge Trail and continue another 0.25 mile to the upper falls. (The hill drops away steeply here, but the trail is wide.) Here's where the trail leads behind the falls in a cavelike cleft in the basalt.

From the upper falls, the trail rolls along, offering views of the Columbia and the Washington side of the gorge. At about 0.8 mile the trail starts to drop and soon provides a view down into steep-walled Oneonta Gorge. Switchback down to a bridge crossing Oneonta Creek, listening for the roar of Lower Oneonta Falls below, then head back up briefly to a junction with Horse Creek Trail.

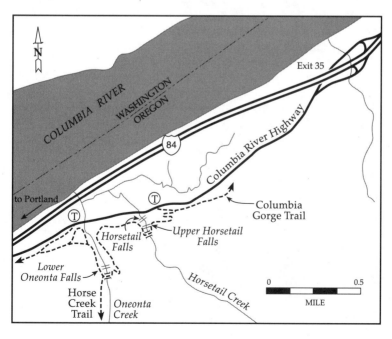

Continue west on Columbia Gorge Trail. Proceed another 0.75 mile or so to the last trail junction, head down and east, and follow above the highway, dropping slowly to eventually meet it.

Finish the hike with a 0.5 mile trek back up the old highway to your car. Take care; the road shoulder is narrow in places, but cars on the old highway tend to poke along slowly. Be sure to pause at the mouth of Oneonta Gorge for a different perspective on the chasm already seen from above.

6 WAHCLELLA FALLS

Type ■ Day hike
Difficulty ■ Easy for children
Distance ■ 2 miles round trip
Terrain ■ 340 feet elevation gain
High point ■ 380 feet
Hikable ■ Most of the year
Contact ■ Columbia River Gorge National Scenic Area, (541) 386-2333

Waterfalls small and large, a gaping creek canyon and boulder garden, and bridges of various sizes all contribute to the charm of this hike, which ends at two-tier Wahclella Falls. At press time, the footbridge that had allowed a loop hike at the end of this trail had been washed away by floods and not yet rebuilt, though the Forest Service was planning to replace it. Whether or not the footbridge is replaced by the time you hike it, you can still access the falls at trail's end via the upper trail, and it's still well worth getting there, though it requires a bit more of a climb.

From Portland take I-84 east to exit 40 (Bonneville); turn right, then right again, following signs a short distance to the cul-de-sac trailhead.

Start hiking on a service road 0.25 mile to a diversion dam, which directs water from Tanner Creek to a downstream fish hatchery. At this point the trail narrows to a footpath along the canyon wall. A wooden footbridge hugs the canyon wall at a waterfall-washed cliff face; notice the basalt columns rising next to the trail. From here the

Horsetail Falls

Wahclella Falls

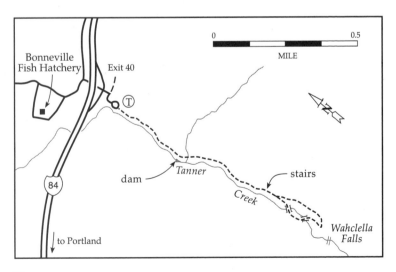

trail starts a steady climb to a wooden staircase at about 0.5 mile. Soon you'll reach a junction. The trail to the right leads to the bridge site; if there's a bridge, cross it and follow the trail upstream across an old rockslide to reach the boisterous falls.

If the bridge is out, continue on the main trail as it climbs, and climbs some more, eventually dropping down to a bouldery falls viewpoint at 1 mile. The falls is a two-tier cataract, dropping perhaps 20 feet to a ledge, then bursting through a rock niche to drop another 60 feet or so into a wide pool. Return as you came, or—if there's a bridge—loop back.

For more fun exploring: Consider a visit to the Bonneville Fish Hatchery, just across the freeway from the trailhead. Trout and sturgeon inhabit the display ponds year-round. There are always some fish in the hatchery raceways, too, but most of the action happens the last week in August through the end of November, when you can watch hatchery workers handling spawning Chinook and coho salmon.

7 EAGLE CREEK

Type ▪ Day hike
Hikable ▪ Most of the year
Contact ▪ Columbia River Gorge National Scenic Area, (541) 386-2333

PUNCHBOWL FALLS
Difficulty ▪ Moderate for children
Distance ▪ 4.2 miles round trip
Terrain ▪ Steady, gentle ascent (280 feet elevation gain)
High point ▪ 400 feet

HIGH BRIDGE
Difficulty ▪ Strenuous for children
Distance ▪ 6.6 miles round trip
Terrain ▪ Steady, gentle ascent (480 feet elevation gain)
High point ▪ 600 feet

Some hikers believe children don't belong on Eagle Creek Trail; they say the trail's too slippery and, in places, too narrow, and the canyon

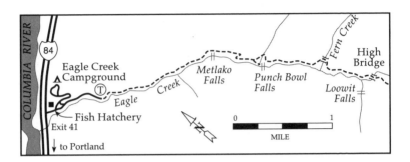

too steep. For others, including Forest Service folks with kids of their own, it's at the top of the list of Columbia Gorge hikes for kids. The upshot: Don't take a large group of young children here (adults do need to keep an eye on them) or individual kids who tend to get out of control, and avoid the trail during rainy spells. Otherwise, it's a gem, with a gentle grade, fine views of steep canyon walls, and even a waterfall or two. Understandably, it's also one of the most popular trails in the gorge.

From Portland take I-84 east to exit 41 (Eagle Creek). Follow the exit road to the fish hatchery, turn right, and follow signs 0.5 mile to the trailhead at the end of the road.

The trail begins as a wide, paved footpath (quickly turning to dirt) following Eagle Creek's east bank. The trail itself gains elevation faster than the creek, however, gradually taking you higher in the basalt-walled canyon. After about 0.75 mile the trail narrows and grows rockier; a steel cable serves as a handrail for about 0.1 mile. Look for the large cave in the basalt cliff across the canyon.

PUNCHBOWL FALLS

After another railed, narrow stretch, the canyon and trail widen, and hikers are surrounded by trees, with the creek out of sight far below but still within earshot. A signed spur trail leads to an overlook for Metlako Falls, about 0.25 mile upstream. At 1.8 mile a spur trail on the right leads to the base of Punch Bowl Falls. It's a steep, rocky, narrow path 0.2 mile down to the creek, but the biggest danger is of a child falling on his or her backside and getting muddy. With a drop of only 10 or 15 feet, the falls isn't dramatic, but it is lovely as it pours into a wide pool. The whole scene—a lushly vegetated basalt grotto—is enchanting and very refreshing on a hot day. Back on the main trail, continue 0.3 mile to a view of Punch Bowl Falls from above.

HIGH BRIDGE

For a longer hike, continue on the main trail another 0.5 mile to
Fern Creek Bridge, a cool picnic spot, and 0.7 mile more to High
Bridge. Here a footbridge crosses the narrow gorge, its creek inky
black in shadows. Just downstream from High Bridge look for Loowit
Falls, which cascades down a sheer rock face into a perfectly round
pool, then fans down the cliff into Eagle Creek. Return as you came
(though the trail continues, linking with trails in Mark O. Hatfield
Wilderness).

Gorge at High Bridge, Eagle Creek Trail

8 CASCADE STREAMWATCH

Type ▪	Day hike
Difficulty ▪	Easy for children
Distance ▪	1.75 miles, loops
Terrain ▪	Nearly level
High point ▪	1200 feet
Hikable ▪	Nearly year-round (road gated in winter; see below)
Contact ▪	Wildwood Recreation Site, (503) 622-3696, in summer; Mount Hood Information Center, (503) 622-7674, year-round

You can't get much more intimate with salmon and steelhead than you can with a hike on a pair of interpretive trails just off US Highway 26, on Mount Hood's west flank. Together they're only 1.75 miles, but they're linked to the Boulder Ridge Trail leading up and

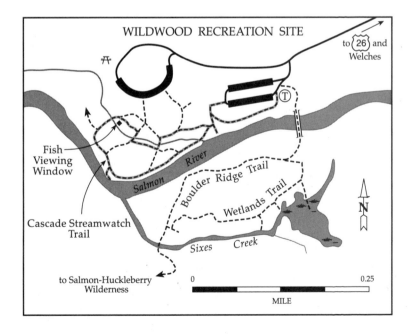

Artwork along Cascade Streamwatch Trail

into Salmon-Huckleberry Wilderness, for hikers who feel they haven't gotten quite enough exercise.

From Portland follow I-84 and US Highway 26 east 40 miles to Welches; turn right at the sign to Wildwood Recreation Site and follow signs 1 mile to the trailhead. The road is gated from November through mid-May, but hikers may park alongside the road and walk in.

The trails lead through forest and marsh past a series of displays beautifully fusing poetry, sculpture, folklore, and science to tell the story of the fishes' life cycle, habitat, and current prospects. Cascade Streamwatch Trail, a three-quarter-mile loop just off the parking area, includes a spur to a covered fish-viewing window set in a moving stream. Cross the river on an arching wooden footbridge to explore the 1-mile Wetlands Trail, with fingers of wooden boardwalk stretching into cattail marsh, beaver pond, and skunk cabbage bog. Oversized, weatherproof naturalists' "journals" provide arty, informative signage at viewing platforms. Follow signs to loop back to your starting point.

If that's not enough exercise, consider a strenuous 2.3-mile, 1400-foot climb to a view of Mount Hood and its forested foothills on Boulder Ridge Trail, which starts off the Wetlands Trail near the footbridge.

9 RAMONA FALLS

Type ■ Day hike
Difficulty ■ Moderate to strenuous for children
Distance ■ 6.9 miles, loop
Terrain ■ 700 feet gradual elevation gain
Hikable ■ May through November
Contact ■ Mount Hood Information Center,
(503) 622-7674

Ramona Falls is the most well-trammeled trail in the Mount Hood Wilderness. Children and adults like the variety the trail offers, including a memorable footbridge; a tall, lacy falls; and a mossy creek gurgling alongside the trail on the walk out. Consider hiking it in the morning, when the sun isn't yet too hot on Old Maid Flat. Following the loop route described here adds to the hike's interest. (For a less-crowded alternative, see Hike 14, Umbrella Falls–Sahalie Falls.)

From US Highway 26 turn north at Zigzag Ranger Station onto Lolo Pass Road (Forest Road 18) and follow it 4.2 miles, turning east onto Forest Road 1825. Continue 2.4 miles and bear left onto Forest Road 100. Follow it 0.5 mile to a huge parking area.

The hike starts with a gentle ascent 1.25 miles to the start of Ramona Falls Trail at a tall footbridge over the Sandy River, milky gray with glacial silt. Immediately you'll reach a junction, the start of the loop route. Hike it counterclockwise to get to the falls a little

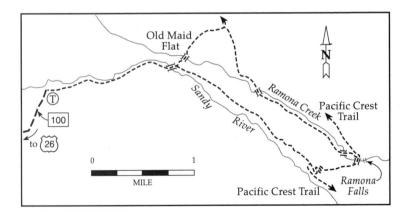

quicker, albeit via a hotter, dustier route. The trail is fairly exposed for the first mile or so, with lodgepole pines lining the route, until it enters a cooler grove of Douglas fir. The river itself is rarely in sight but within hearing distance most of the way.

At 2.8 miles you'll reach the junction with the Pacific Crest Trail (PCT); turn left and continue 0.5 mile to the falls. Standing in front of Ramona Falls on a hot summer's day is like standing in front of an open refrigerator; the lacy veil of water playing down a face of worn columnar basalt is more like 500 miniwaterfalls, each sending cool air into the falls' amphitheaterlike setting. A split-rail fence at the base (and trampled vegetation all around) suggests that visitors enjoy the falls from a distance—a tall order for kids. Instead, direct them toward playing—with supervision—in the creek below the falls.

Mount Hood from Ramona Falls trailhead

The loop route continues past the falls (bear left where the PCT heads right) and down a cool vale following moss-banked Ramona Creek. About 1.5 miles from the falls, you're in hot lodgepole pine country again for most of the way back. About 1.7 miles beyond the falls, near a trail junction, keep a lookout for tree wells, formed about 200 years ago when lava flowed during an eruption of Mount Hood and swirled around standing trees. The wood eventually rotted out, leaving molds where the trees once stood.

At the junction, bear left. In another 0.6 mile, drop down, cross the creek, and arrive at the start of the loop again. Bear right to recross the Sandy River on the high bridge and follow the access trail 1.25 miles back to the parking area.

10 SALMON RIVER

Type ■ Day hike or backpack
Hikable ■ Most of the year
Contact ■ Mount Hood Information Center,
(503) 622-7674

LOWER TRAIL
Difficulty ■ Easy for children
Distance: ■ 2.6 miles one way
Terrain ■ Nearly level (gains 120 feet)
High point ■ 1,640 feet

WILDERNESS TRAIL
Difficulty ■ Moderate for children
Distance ■ 4.4 miles round trip (or more)
Terrain ■ Gradual ascent (260 feet elevation gain)
High point ■ 1900 feet

Though it threads a narrow corridor between the road and river and isn't exactly remote, the Old Salmon River Trail has a particular charm for families with children. It's wide and virtually level and offers a lot of river access. The huge trees of the old-growth forest it traverses are a big part of the trail's appeal. It's also accessible from many points along the road, so you can easily make short, one-way hikes with a second car, possibly a child's first backpack trip to one of several campsites along the trail. If you're after more of a hike, pick

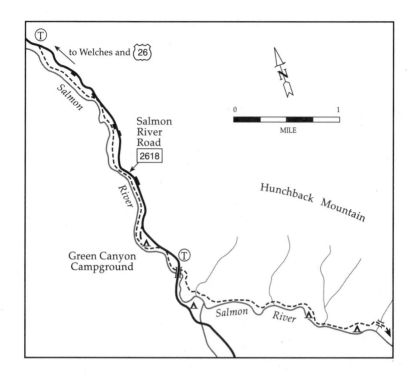

up the Salmon River Trail where the "old" trail ends and follow it into Salmon-Huckleberry Wilderness.

Traveling east on US Highway 26 about 40 miles from Portland, turn right onto Salmon River Road (Forest Road 2618) just west of Zigzag Ranger Station and follow it 2.8 miles to the lower trailhead. The end of Old Salmon River Trail and the beginning of the wilderness section of trail are 2.3 miles farther along this road, at the concrete bridge crossing the river.

LOWER TRAIL

Beginning at the northernmost trailhead, follow the trail upstream. There are huge, gorgeous Douglas firs and sword ferns alongside the trail, little footbridges to cross, and lacy cedars sweeping overhead. Bleeding hearts and oxalis carpet the forest floor. The Salmon River itself is particularly appealing on hot summer days, for anglers and others; it's deep green, alternating between deep pools and rocky riffles. Watch wading children carefully, as it is a river with a substantial current.

Old Salmon River Trail

About a mile from the trailhead, bear right at an apparent fork (and at most other apparent forks; these are generally spurs leading back to the road). At 1.4 miles, the main trail itself leads out to the road at a point where the road is too close to the river to allow room for the trail. Walk along the road for 0.1 mile until the trail resumes and reenters the woods along the river. After walking through a portion of Green Canyon Campground, briefly wind up back along the road once more, 0.3 mile before the concrete bridge that signals the end of the lower trail stretch.

WILDERNESS TRAIL

From the concrete bridge past Green Canyon Campground, the trail immediately starts climbing then drops to a bend in the river at 0.3 mile—a great picnic and exploring spot, and possibly swimming for the brave in midsummer. The trail continues to gradually ascend the deep forest, with huge trees trail-side. A good turnaround spot with kids is the side creek footbridge at 2.2 miles; beyond this point the trail moves away from the river. Back at 2 miles you'll find several campsites, but they're popular with backpackers in late spring and early summer and are first-come, first-served. If you do camp here, be especially careful about sanitation and use designated "toilet areas." The trail continues into the wilderness, linking with other trails in Salmon-Huckleberry Wilderness. Return as you came.

11 LITTLE ZIGZAG FALLS

Type ▪	Day hike
Difficulty ▪	Easy for children
Distance ▪	1 mile round trip
Terrain ▪	Nearly level
High point ▪	3200 feet
Hikable ▪	Most of the year
Contact ▪	Mount Hood Information Center, (503) 622-7674

This is an ideal first hike for very young children on a visit to Mount Hood. It's just a few minutes' drive off US Highway 26, it's virtually

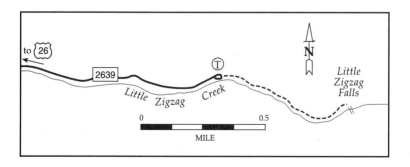

Little Zigzag Falls

level and not very long, and it ends at a lovely falls. Kids will enjoy wandering the easy path through the forest and playing by the pool at the base of the falls.

Traveling east on US Highway 26, drive 6 miles past Zigzag Ranger Station and turn left onto Forest Road 2639. Drive 1.3 miles to the signed trailhead and large parking turnout (the road is blocked to further travel at this point).

The well-constructed trail follows alongside icy, clear, swift Little Zigzag Creek through a lush, narrow canyon. Listen closely to the sounds the creek makes as it tumbles over rocks and logs and flows along sandy shallows; you can almost hear it converse with itself in different voices. Look for skunk cabbage in spring and blooming rhododendrons in early summer.

The base of Little Zigzag Falls is about 0.5 mile from the trailhead. Stand on the viewpoint—a structure built of rocks piled inside a cylinder of wire fencing—to watch the falls tumble about 75 feet in a series of short drops at the top, then one long cascade down an angled, mossy, chiseled rock face. The trail continues, making one switchback to climb to the top of the falls, where it ends. Return as you came.

12 MIRROR LAKE

Type ▪	Day hike or backpack
Difficulty ▪	Moderate for children
Distance ▪	3.2 miles, loop
Terrain ▪	700 feet elevation gain
High point ▪	4100 feet
Hikable ▪	May through October
Contact ▪	Mount Hood Information Center, (503) 622-7674

This is one of the busiest trails on Mount Hood, for obvious reasons: It's relatively close to Portland and just the right length for a moderately easy hike, and the reward is a classic view of Mount Hood towering above Mirror Lake. Even on a weekday you probably won't be alone, so take particular care to have as little impact as possible by staying on the trail, keeping voices low at the lake, and scrupulously picking up after yourself. Consider hiking here in early summer, when the rhododendrons and bear grass are in bloom.

From Government Camp drive 2 miles west on US Highway 26 to the trailhead on the south side of the highway. Cross Camp Creek on a footbridge and start up the trail, which immediately passes several big tree stumps with springboard cuts, evidence of old-time logging.

Walk through Douglas fir, cedar, and pine forest for the first 0.5 mile, then cross a scree slope that seems to house a colony of little, furry pikas (listen for their call). Back in the woods, look for more springboard-cut stumps while switchbacking up toward the lake. The far-off sound of eighteen-wheelers grinding up the highway accompanies hikers most of the way along the trail, until the trail drops into the lake basin.

Mount Hood from Mirror Lake

At 1.4 miles you'll meet the lake's gurgling outlet creek on the left and a trail junction, the start of a 0.4-mile loop trail around the lake. A sign indicates that campsites are to the right, and that's also the fastest route to the best lakeside picnic sites. The right fork arrives at the lake in just 0.1 mile.

Rough stairs lead to nice picnic sites on this side of the lake. A short distance farther, the trail splits. The left fork continues around the lake, granting postcard views of Mount Hood. It follows a log boardwalk across the lake's boggy inlet and continues to the trail junction near its outlet.

The right fork leads steadily up another 1.6 miles (and 800 feet in elevation) to the top of Tom Dick and Harry Mountain, a worthwhile extension of the hike for older children after a pause at the lake. The trail here is less used and hence a bit rougher.

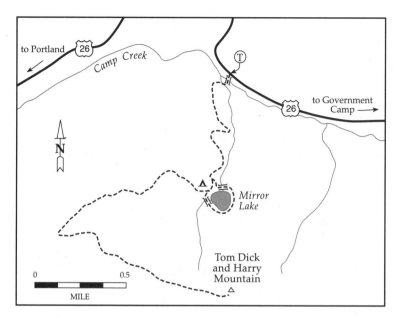

 13 TIMBERLINE TRAILS

Type ▪ Day hike
Hikable ▪ July through October
Contact ▪ Mount Hood Information Center,
(503) 622-7674

WHITE RIVER CANYON OVERLOOK

Difficulty ▪ Easy for children
Distance ▪ 1 mile round trip
Terrain ▪ Steady ascent (100 feet elevation gain)
High point ▪ 5900 feet

ZIGZAG CANYON OVERLOOK

Difficulty ▪ Moderate for children
Distance ▪ 4.4 miles round trip
Terrain ▪ Level or steady ascent (500 feet
elevation gain)
High point ▪ 5900 feet

A trip to Timberline Lodge is worthwhile any time of year: it's blanketed in snow in winter or surrounded by a profusion of wildflowers in summer. The round-the-mountain Timberline Trail (here part of the Pacific Crest Trail) passes right above the lodge, urging visitors out for an alpine hike.

From the east end of Government Camp (55 miles east of Portland on US Highway 26), turn left up the road to Timberline Lodge, at the end of the 6-mile road. The modern building below is the day lodge, with a gift shop and other visitor services. Above is grand old (1938) Timberline Lodge itself. Peruse the historical exhibits on the first floor and take a turn through the high-ceilinged great room on the second floor.

WHITE RIVER CANYON OVERLOOK

For a short—but steep—walk, go east on the trail outside the lodge, heading up; it connects with the main Timberline Trail in about 0.25 mile, then reaches a view into White River Canyon at about 0.5 mile, at which point the trail starts a long descent. Return as you came.

ZIGZAG CANYON OVERLOOK

For a longer hike follow signs west from the lodge, ducking under a chair lift and into the trees. You'll pass through a succession of dazzling alpine meadows. At 1 mile, after connecting with the main Timberline Trail, the route dives down into rocky Little Zigzag Canyon (a possible turnaround point), climbs back out, descends through

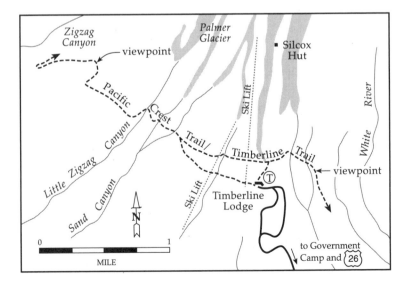

Mount Hood from Timberline Trail

forest and meadow, then climbs to a grand view overlooking Zigzag Canyon and—on clear days—an array of peaks to the south. Return as you came.

For more fun exploring: The Magic Mile and Palmer chair lifts operate through Labor Day for skiers as well as visitors on foot (fee charged). Consider riding up and hiking the 2 miles back down, possibly with a side trip to Silcox Hut, just east of the top of the Magic Mile lift. The old mountain chalet—first the terminus for the original Magic Mile chair lift, later a rustic hut for climbers—has been restored and now offers limited food service for drop-in visitors as well as lodging by reservation (mostly for groups).

14 UMBRELLA FALLS–SAHALIE FALLS

Type ▪ Day hike
Difficulty ▪ Moderate for children
Distance ▪ 4.1 miles, loop
Terrain ▪ Steady ascents (800 feet elevation gain)
High point ▪ 5240 feet
Hikable ▪ June through October
Contact ▪ Mount Hood Information Center,
(503) 622-7674

Summer hikes don't get much better than this. Early in the season the trail is lined with pale-green huckleberry leaves and white bear grass plumes; later the meadows are ablaze with wildflowers. Just about when the flower show starts to fade, the huckleberries ripen. Then

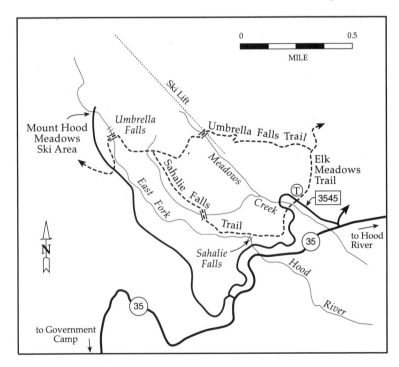

East Fork Hood River below Umbrella Falls

there are the waterfalls and the views. The novelty of hiking across the ski runs at Mount Hood Meadows is titillating for children who ski or snowboard here in the winter. Although there are various ways to hike part or all of the trails around Hood River Meadows, this loop route makes a good, varied, moderate day hike for families.

From Government Camp follow US Highway 26 east about 3 miles to the junction with State Highway 35. Follow State 35 east about 7 miles and turn left at the sign to Hood River Meadows on Forest Road 3545 (about a mile east of the turnoff to Mount Hood Meadows ski area). Drive 0.4 mile and park in a turnout at the trailhead for Sahalie Falls Trail. For a clockwise loop, start hiking on the left side of the road.

With all the huckleberries at the trailhead in late August or early September, it may be hard to get a group started up the trail; assure them there's a lot more ahead. The trail crosses a boggy area on a log, then leads to a creek that is crossed on rocks. Follow the creek up to a road, cross it, then continue up to Sahalie Falls, off the main trail to the left at 0.5 mile.

Back on the main trail, climb uphill steadily, following the East Fork Hood River's east bank. At about 1 mile descend momentarily to cross a creek, then resume the climb, passing more little creeks and traversing some meadows. At 1.7 miles the trail reaches a T junction with Umbrella Falls Trail. Turn left and walk 0.3 mile to Umbrella Falls, also on the East Fork Hood River. The exceptionally pretty falls is a great destination for lunch or playtime. A bridge crosses the wide, sandy creek below the falls, which streams gently down a rounded rock face like rain down an umbrella. An asphalt path leads 0.2 mile to the top of the falls; continue a few steps farther to reach the lower end of the Mount Hood Meadows parking area.

To resume the hike from Umbrella Falls, return 0.3 mile to the junction and continue straight. About 0.2 mile from the junction the trail emerges from the forest and begins traversing a wide meadow (a ski run) with a great mountain view. The trail passes under a ski lift and continues in and out of forest and meadow for about a mile before reentering the forest. After about 0.2 mile in the woods, bear right at the three-way junction with Elk Meadows Trail. Continue another 0.4 mile back to the trailhead.

15 TAMAWANAS FALLS

Type ▪ Day hike
Difficulty ▪ Moderate for children
Distance ▪ 4.2 miles round trip
Terrain ▪ 360 feet elevation gain
High point ▪ 3400 feet
Hikable ▪ May through October
Contact ▪ Mount Hood Information Center, (503) 622-7674

Four wooden footbridges that surely shelter trolls, a butterfly-shaped waterfall, a steep talus slope: This trail packs a whole lot of interest per mile. All the trail-side attractions (and the anticipation of more) help the miles speed by.

From Hood River drive south on State Highway 35 about 25 miles and pull over at the trailhead, marked by a sign for East Fork Trail, on the west side of the road. From Government Camp follow US

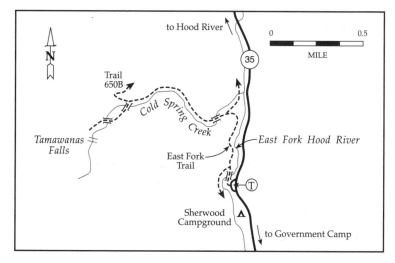

Highway 26 east about 8 miles to the junction with State 35, then follow State 35 east and north about 14 miles to the trailhead, which is just north of Sherwood Campground.

Walk through the campground toward milky-colored East Fork Hood River and cross it on a narrow log bridge. Two-tier railings make the bridge relatively safe for children, but you'll want to watch them closely just the same. At the end of the bridge, bear right. The trail heads north for a rather unappealing 0.6 mile, following above the river and in sight of the highway. It bears left and meets a trail junction (go straight), and things improve quickly. The trail drops into the cool canyon of Cold Spring Creek, crosses the creek, and heads up the noisy, moss-banked stream. Encourage the kids to get down on their knees to examine tiny bunchberry and twinflower blossoms or—later in the season—their berries (inedible).

Continue upstream on the rather rocky trail, rounding a big boulder at about 1.5 miles. Walk along the bottom of a scree slope past a junction with Trail 650B, then recross the creek on a log bridge. Switchback up the canyon a couple of times, drop down some steps, and cross the creek for the last time. This is a lovely spot—pool above, frothy drops below—and a good place for a snack before the final push to the falls. It's only about 0.25 mile up (and up) some switchbacks and around the hill to a view of Tamawanas Falls at the trail's end. The falls drop about 100 feet through a depression worn in a cliff of columnar basalt. Cliffs fan out like butterfly wings on either side of the stream of water. Return as you came.

Tamawanas Falls

16 LITTLE CRATER LAKE

Type ▪ Day hike
Difficulty ▪ Easy for children
Distance to Little Crater Lake ▪ 0.4 mile round trip
Distance to Crater Creek ▪ 1.2 miles round trip
Terrain ▪ Level
High point ▪ 3250 feet
Hikable ▪ May through October
Contact ▪ Mount Hood Information Center, (503) 622-7674

Little it is: a jewel of a pond, its color an iridescent blue-green. The paved path to the lake leads through a moist meadow blooming all summer with a succession of wildflowers; the tall stalks of white-blossomed hellebore held sway on our last visit. From Little Crater Lake it's just a few more minutes to Crater Creek, perfect for dipping toes on a hot day. At this point you're on the Pacific Crest Trail (PCT), with plenty of options to extend the day's hike.

 From the junction of State Highway 35 and US Highway 26 at Mount Hood, take US 26 south about 9 miles and turn right at the

sign to Timothy Lake (Forest Road 42). Follow it 4.2 miles and turn
right at the sign to Little Crater Lake (Forest Road 58). In 2.3 miles
turn left into Little Crater Campground and follow the road around
to the signed trailhead at the edge of the meadow.

Follow the paved path through the meadow, into a grove of trees,
and to the wooden platform at the edge of Little Crater Lake. Signs
explain how the lake came to be—nothing like the process that produced big Crater Lake. Rather, hundreds of years ago water was
forced up through a crack in a fault line, creating an artesian spring,
washing away the sandstone under the meadow, and creating a small
but deep (45 feet at one point) lake.

Continue around the right side of the lake on the trail to hook up
with the PCT in another 0.1 mile. Turn left (south) and continue 0.3
mile to another junction, the start of a loop trail around Timothy
Lake. Bear left (staying on the PCT); immediately you'll come to a
wooden bridge crossing shallow, 50-foot-wide Crater Creek. Its
sandy bottom invites wading on hot days. Return as you came.

Check a forest map to consider longer hike options, including a
one-way hike with shuttle car to Oak Fork Campground (4.5 miles),
the first of several campgrounds on the south shore of Timothy Lake.

For more fun exploring: Take a side trip about 5 miles down Forest
Road 42 to Clackamas Historical Ranger Station, a restored 1930s
log ranger station alongside the Oak Grove Fork of the Clackamas
River. It's been period-furnished, from the potbelly stove to the photo
of FDR over the desk, and now serves as a living museum and information center.

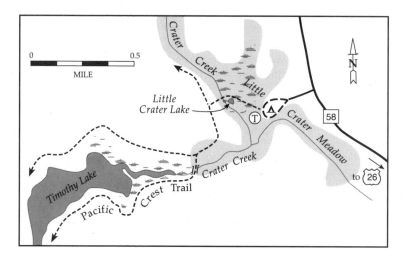

Little Crater Lake

17 BAGBY HOT SPRINGS

Type	Day hike or backpack
Difficulty	Easy for children
Distance	3 miles round trip
Terrain	Gentle ascent (190 feet elevation gain)
High point	2272 feet
Hikable	Most of the year
Contact	Estacada Ranger District, (503) 630-6861

Big wood-stave tubs and narrow baths carved of single logs capture the sulphur-scented hot water that bubbles out of the ground near the Hot Springs Fork of the Collawash River—a welcome treat, especially when hiking in the cool of late fall or early spring (or even midwinter, if snowpack permits). Bagby is a "clothing optional" spot; some visitors bathe with swimsuits, others in the buff. Hikers uncomfortable with public nudity should choose another hike. Otherwise, Bagby can be great fun with kids. They'll enjoy exploring the hot and cold springs, the old guard station, and the bathing facilities.

The water emerges at 136 degrees Fahrenheit; prime the tub with a few buckets of cold water first. Bagby is always crowded on weekends and often on weekdays as well, so the best bet is to go on a weekday first thing in the morning, preferably in spring or fall.

From Estacada follow State Highway 224 southeast 26 miles to Ripplebrook Ranger Station. Continue 0.5 mile past the ranger station and bear right onto Forest Road 46. In 3.6 miles turn right onto Forest Road 63. In another 3.6 miles turn right onto Forest Road 70. Continue 6 miles to the large trailhead parking area, on the left.

From the trailhead follow an asphalt path 30 yards to a long log bridge over Nohorn Creek. After the bridge the trail becomes a wide dirt path, level or gently ascending through old-growth forest. At about 0.6 mile the trail meets and follows alongside the Hot Springs Fork of the Collawash River. Plank boardwalks or raised trail sections help hikers over boggy spots here and there. At 1.25 miles the trail crosses the Hot Springs Fork on another tall, skinny bridge at a

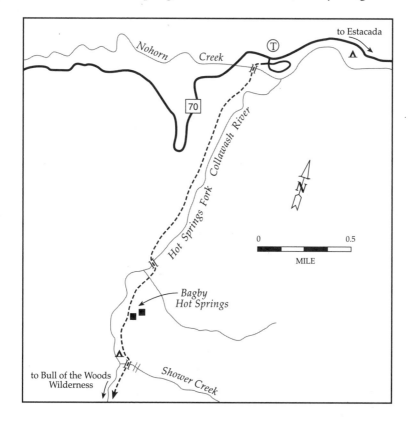

Snack time at Bagby Hot Springs

dramatic point where a huge boulder splits the river into two chutes. From there, the trail ascends gently for the final 0.25 mile to the springs and main bathhouse, on the left.

Some tubs are in enclosed bathhouses, others are open to the woods and other bathers. You may have to wait your turn for a tub. Up the trail and off to the left a bit (beyond the old guard station) is another tub and, near it, a bubbling hot spring that feeds it; kids will enjoy exploring here (the spring feeding the main bathhouse is fenced off).

Overnight camping is not permitted right at the springs; rather, camp 0.3 mile up the trail along the river at Shower Creek. Day hikers may enjoy extending their visit with a walk to the falls at Shower Creek or farther. The trail enters Bull of the Woods Wilderness 0.6 mile beyond Bagby and continues in deep forest. Return as you came.

18 PANSY LAKE

Type	Day hike or backpack
Difficulty	Easy for children
Distance	2.6 miles round trip
Terrain	Steady ascent (450 feet elevation gain)
High point	3994 feet
Hikable	June through October
Contact	Estacada Ranger District, (503) 630-6861

The hike to Pansy Lake is perhaps a little tougher than that to Bagby Hot Springs (Hike 17)—steeper, though shorter—and a lot less

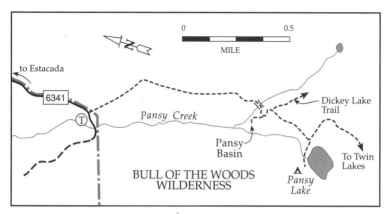

crowded. There are campsites at the lake, but equally appealing for overnighting is Pansy Basin, a short detour on an unmaintained spur off the lake trail. The prolific bear grass bloom along the trail usually reaches its peak in late June.

From Estacada follow State Highway 224 southeast 26 miles to Ripplebrook Ranger Station. Continue 0.5 mile past the ranger station and bear right onto Forest Road 46. In 3.6 miles turn right onto Forest Road 63. Follow it 5.7 miles (passing the turnoff to the Bagby Hot Springs trailhead, Hike 17) and turn right on Forest Road 6340. Drive 8 miles, then bear right on Forest Road 6341; continue 3.6 miles to a wide turnout on the right and park. (If there is no trail sign, look for a sign indicating the end of road maintenance.) The trail starts across the road to the left of a small creek.

Pansy Lake

Immediately the trail passes a sign indicating the start of Bull of the Woods Wilderness. The trail climbs steadily most of the way through deep forest, crossing first a small stream and then a larger one, both on steppingstones. At 0.9 mile an unsigned spur trail on the right leads downhill a short distance to Pansy Basin, an open, grassy meadow inviting for young backpackers. Just up the main trail, pass a junction with the Dickey Lake Trail, on the left. At 1.2 miles the trail levels off at a fork, with the trail to Twin Lakes heading left and Pansy Lake a hop, skip, and a jump to the right.

Follow the lake spur along the water's edge, passing a small campsite and crossing the lake's outlet creek on a narrow log. There's a larger campsite and a pleasant little beach just beyond the creek, where the trail ends. Return as you came.

19 RUSS LAKE

Type	▪ Day hike or backpack
Difficulty	▪ Easy for children
Distance	▪ 1.6 miles round trip
Terrain	▪ Very gentle ascent (100 feet elevation gain)
High point	▪ 4600 feet
Hikable	▪ June through September
Contact	▪ Estacada Ranger District, (503) 630-6861

Most Willamette Valley residents would consider the Olallie Lakes Scenic Area too far a drive for a day trip. Instead, make it a destination for a weekend or week of high-mountain hiking and boating. Take along a canoe, or rent a rowboat at Olallie Lake Resort. No motorboats are permitted, adding to the pristine feel of the area. Many of the lakes are air-stocked every year; fishing is best in June and September.

Hikers can choose from a dozen or so day-hike routes in the immediate area. Russ Lake and Fish Lake, Hike 20, are the only two in this book. For information on others, call the Forest Service number above. Russ Lake Trail touches three lakes, though it intersects other trails, creating options for extending a hike. All three lakes have good fishing, though these and other lakes east of Olallie and Monon Lakes are on the Warm Springs Indian Reservation and require a tribal permit for fishing; (541) 553-1161.

Olallie Butte beyond Russ Lake

From Salem take State Highway 22 east to Detroit. Turn north onto Forest Road 46 at the sign to Breitenbush. Continue 23.7 miles to Forest Road 4690 and turn right. (From Portland, take State Highway 211 to Estacada, then follow State Highway 224 for 26 miles to Ripplebrook Ranger Station. Turn south on Forest Road 46 and follow it for 25 miles to Forest Road 4690.) Take Forest Road 4690 (turns to gravel in 7.7 miles) south 8.2 miles, turn right onto Skyline Road (Forest Road 4220), drive 1.4 miles, and turn left at Olallie Meadow Campground. Park at the trailhead parking area at the end of the campground.

The trail starts at the edge of lovely, broad Olallie Meadow and heads immediately into the trees on a narrow path lined with bear grass and huckleberry. At 0.2 mile turn left at the junction with Lodgepole Trail. Soon the trail starts to climb gently; at 0.4 mile a spur to the left leads a short distance up to charming little Brook Lake.

Continuing up the main trail, it reaches the junction with the Pacific Crest Trail (PCT) at 0.5 mile; for a side trip to Jude Lake, turn left onto the PCT and walk 0.2 mile to the lake's northwest corner. Jude Lake is another charmer, with a campsite near the shore (a sign points the way). Back on the main trail, it's another 0.3 mile to Russ Lake, passing the southeast end of Jude Lake along the way. The big, green, and round Russ Lake is definitely the prize on this hike. Olallie Butte looms across the water. For true luxury, pack in a small raft and spend the day floating and trolling.

For more fun exploring: If the kids like this hike and are ready for more of the same, try the similar, but more challenging, Red Lakes

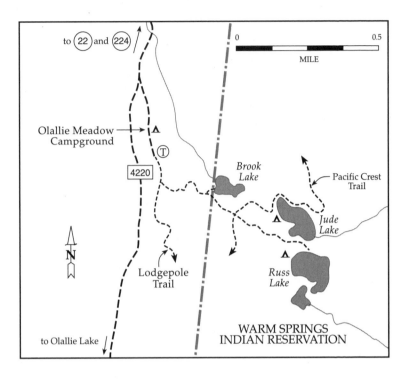

Trail. It starts just south of Olallie Guard Station and hits Top Lake at 1.3 miles, Sheep Lake at 2.8 miles, and three more lakes spaced no more than 0.5 mile apart.

20 FISH LAKE

Type ■	Day hike or backpack
Difficulty ■	Moderate for children
Distance ■	3.2 miles round trip
Terrain ■	From level to steady ascent (420 feet elevation gain)
High point ■	4900 feet
Hikable ■	June through September
Contact ■	Estacada Ranger District, (503) 630-6861

There are trailheads at either end of Fish Lake Trail, but the dramatic approach to Fish Lake from the south is a good argument for starting at the southern trailhead. Besides, this trailhead is closer for families camping in the area. You could make this a one-way, downhill, 2.8-mile hike, but the long car shuttle required makes it hard to justify.

From Salem take State Highway 22 east to Detroit. Turn north onto Forest Road 46 at the sign to Breitenbush. Continue 23.7 miles to Forest Road 4690 and turn right. (From Portland, take State Highway 211 to Estacada, then follow State Highway 224 for 26 miles to Ripplebrook Ranger Station. Turn south on Forest Road 46 and follow it for 25 miles to Forest Road 4690.) Take Forest Road 4690 (turns to gravel in 7.7 miles) south 8.2 miles, turn right onto Skyline Road (Forest Road 4220), drive 4.5 miles (past Olallie Meadow Campground) to Lower Lake Campground.

The trail starts level, then descends gently to reach Lower Lake at 0.3 mile. Follow along the lakeshore, passing a nice little gravel beach. The bank is sharp, but there are plenty of appealing places to pause for a snack or some rock tossing. At 0.6 mile the trail passes a pleasant campsite at a shallow cove at the lake's far end.

Cross the lake's outlet creek and go straight across the junction with Lodgepole Trail. There the trail starts dropping, through a jungle of bear grass and huckleberry, to reach a magnificent view of Fish Lake, nearly 200 feet below, at 1 mile. Savvy kids may have second thoughts about hiking down that far (knowing they'll eventually have to hike back up); let them know that it's not all that far, that switchbacks make the grade pretty moderate, and that they can take

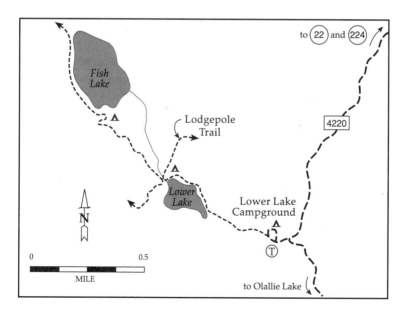

Fish Lake

their time on the return. Begin the plunge down to the lake, through an old-growth forest, down four switchbacks, and across a creek on midstream rocks, to reach the pretty lakeshore at 1.6 miles. There's an appealing campsite near the lake, and trout fishing is usually good in June and September.

For more fun exploring: Rent a rowboat at Olallie Lake Resort; all of the lakes in this area are off limits to motorboats. Or consider a hike around one of the bigger lakes. Trails circumscribe both Olallie and adjacent Monon Lake; Monon Lake (3.8 miles around, including 0.2 mile on gravel road) is more remote, and you can swim in it (but not in Olallie, a drinking water source). Start at the boat ramp at Peninsula Campground, 2 miles south of the road to Lower Lake Campground on Skyline Road.

Footbridge across the McKenzie River

CASCADES
TO THE COAST
RANGE

21 MCDOWELL CREEK FALLS

Type ▪ Day hike
Difficulty ▪ Easy for children
Distance ▪ 1.7 miles, loop
Terrain ▪ Some short, steep ascents (200 feet elevation gain)
High point ▪ 1000 feet
Hikable ▪ Year-round
Contact ▪ Linn County Parks, (541) 967-3917

If it weren't for Silver Falls State Park (Hike 22), 25 miles north as the crow flies, you'd know all about McDowell Creek Park and its dazzling waterfalls. This small county park and its cataract-filled canyon isn't quite on the scale of the canyon at Silver Falls. But in less than 2 miles you can see three major waterfalls, from 20 to 119 feet tall.

From I-5, south of Albany, take US Highway 20 east about 10 miles to Lebanon. Continue on US 20 another 4 miles, and turn left at the sign to McDowell Creek Park. Follow signs another 10 miles into the park.

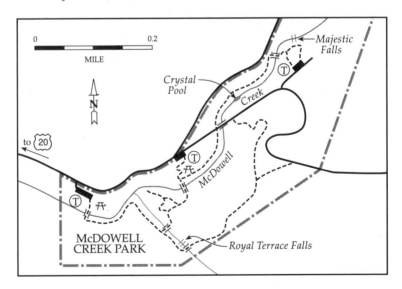

Boardwalk and trail below Majestic Falls

You can drive to within a few steps of two of the falls: 119-foot Royal Terrace Falls and 39-foot Majestic Falls. But with just 0.2 mile of roadside walking and the same amount of trail backtracking, you can make a loop trip. Park at the first of three parking areas and take the trail to the base of Royal Terrace Falls, on a side creek. At the trail junction turn left, crossing a footbridge, and follow the trail (bearing left at all junctions) through the forest, over the road, and back into the forest to 20-foot Crystal Pool. Wooden stairs lead up the canyon to a large viewing platform at Majestic Falls, and stone steps lead to the uppermost parking area. Walk back down the road 0.2 mile and take the unmarked trail on the left, just before the road crosses the creek. It leads back to Royal Terrace Falls and your car.

22 SILVER CREEK CANYON

Type ▪ Day hike
Hikeable ▪ Year-round
FYI ▪ No dogs allowed (except on Ridge Trail)
Contact ▪ Silver Falls State Park, (503) 873-8681

SOUTH FALLS–RIDGE TRAIL LOOP
Difficulty ▪ Moderate for children
Distance ▪ 2.3 miles, loop
Terrain ▪ Steady ascent (440 feet elevation gain)
High point ▪ 1320 feet

SOUTH FALLS–WINTER FALLS LOOP
Difficulty ▪ Moderate to strenuous for children
Distance ▪ 3 miles, loop
Terrain ▪ Steady ascent (960 feet elevation gain)
High point ▪ 1320 feet

NORTH FALLS–WINTER FALLS LOOP
Difficulty ▪ Moderate for children
Distance ▪ 3 miles, loop
Terrain ▪ Steady ascent (380 feet elevation gain)
High point ▪ 1490 feet

Silver Falls State Park is one of Oregon's premier family parks, with hiking trails, paved bicycle paths, equestrian trails, and a great campground, all in a magnificent forested canyon with ten major waterfalls—and less than a half-hour from I-5. The configuration of trails offers numerous options, from short falls-viewing jaunts to longer loops.

You can see all ten falls in a 7-mile loop starting at South Falls (or the quieter North Falls Day Use Area). Here are three, kid-friendly, short loop options, which are further described below: South Falls to Lower South Falls, returning on the Ridge Trail (two waterfalls); South Falls to Winter Falls (six waterfalls); and North Falls to Winter Falls (three waterfalls). Hikes here never seem long—surprises wait around the corner—but there's no denying the long climb back from the canyon floor. The park is appealing in all seasons, even winter, when subfreezing temperatures nearly freeze the falls in place.

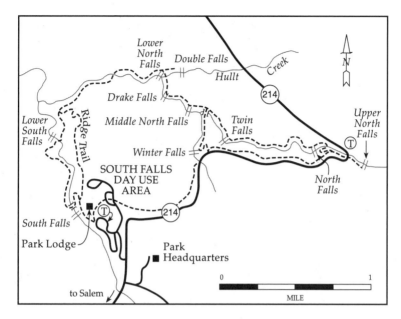

But mist from the falls coats the trails with ice, too, so tour the frozen waterfalls with great care.

From I-5 near Salem take exit 253 and follow State Highway 22 southeast 5 miles to State Highway 214. Drive east 16.5 miles on State 214, follow signs to the park, and turn left into South Falls Day Use Area. Follow signs to Picnic Area C and park at the far end of the lot. Follow the paved path past the rest rooms a short distance to a low stone wall overlooking South Falls. The North Falls Day Use Area parking is another 2.3 miles east and north on State 214 through the park.

SOUTH FALLS–RIDGE TRAIL LOOP

From the viewpoint overlooking 177-foot South Falls, follow signs to the paved path leading to the base of the falls. Turn left at the junction to walk behind the falls. Follow the path down to the footbridge at the base of the falls. Cross it for a short loop back to the parking lot; otherwise, continue down the creek's west bank on the now unpaved (and often rocky and muddy) trail. In 0.7 mile you will see 93-foot Lower South Falls just before the trail plunges down 187 steps and winds behind the falls. Continue 0.3 mile to a junction; bear right to take the 1-mile Ridge Trail up and out of the canyon and back to your car.

SOUTH FALLS–WINTER FALLS LOOP

Begin as you did for the shorter loop, above. At the junction with the Ridge Trail, however, continue on the main trail. When next you see the creek, note that it seems to be flowing backward. What happened? You've passed the confluence with the north fork of Silver Creek and are now following it upstream.

Just past Lower North Falls take the short spur up Hullt Creek to see tall, skinny Double Falls. At Middle North Falls, a spur leads behind the falls, but it's narrow, rough, very slick, and best avoided with kids. To complete the loop, turn right over the footbridge 0.2 mile past Middle North Falls and follow a dainty side creek to the base of Winter Falls. Continue to the top of the falls, emerging at a small highway turnout. The trail resumes on the far side of the turnout, staying parallel to the road for about 0.5 mile (and converging briefly with a bicycle path a couple of times) before heading off into lovely old-growth forest.

When the trail meets the road, cross the road, pick up the trail again, and continue a short distance to a parking lot. Cross it, then follow a paved service road to the park's lodge. Walk past the lodge, then past the rest rooms, and arrive back at the hike's start.

NORTH FALLS–WINTER FALLS LOOP

From the parking area above North Falls, cross the arching footbridge, bear left where a spur splits off to the right back under the bridge, then bear right at the next fork. In a few minutes the trail reaches the top of North Falls. Continue along the railed, cliff-hugging trail, then down seventy-eight steps and back behind the falls in a wide, deep, dry cave. The sound of the falls pounding the rocks below reverberates in the cave, sounding like a jumbo jet at take-off. Walk with care; seeping water makes the trail slick in places. Continue downstream about 1 mile to Twin Falls, passing a huge, split boulder resting in the creek. Past Twin Falls, turn left across the north fork on a footbridge and follow a side creek up to Winter Falls. At the top of the falls, the trail reaches a highway turnout; the trail resumes on the left, following close to the road 1 mile back to the arching footbridge at the hike's start. Return to your car, or walk under the footbridge (and road bridge) and take a side trail another 0.2 mile upstream to see Upper North Falls, then return as you came.

Lower South Falls

23 OPAL CREEK

Type ▪	Day hike or backpack
Difficulty ▪	Strenuous for children
Distance ▪	7.2 miles round trip
Terrain ▪	Rolling (280 feet elevation gain)
High point ▪	2200 feet
Hikable ▪	Nearly year-round
Contact ▪	Detroit Ranger District, (503) 854-3366

After a long battle, the renowned old-growth forest here finally won wilderness protection in 1998. Hikers used to have to follow an old road 3.2 miles to the old mining camp at Jawbone Flats just to begin a trip into the fabled forest here. Now a trail gets you off the road after 2.2 miles and leads to a view of dazzling, emerald-green Opal Pool. The long walk to the pool, while scenic, may be too monotonous to interest younger hikers—the primary reason for the strenuous difficulty rating.

 From I-5 at Salem take State Highway 22 east 23 miles. East of Mehama 1 mile, turn left on Little North Fork Road (becomes Forest Road 2209 where it enters the national forest) and follow it

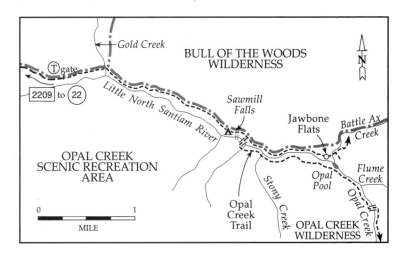

Jawbone Flats

for 21 miles (the last 5.5 miles are gravel). Park where a gate blocks further access.

Continue on foot up the old road, crossing Gold Creek, passing through younger forest, then beginning at about 1.75 miles traversing some of prettiest old growth of the hike, with huge Douglas firs as much as 7 and 8 feet in diameter. At 2 miles there's a collection of old machinery and a campsite where a primitive lumber mill operated a half-century ago, and behind it, a swimming hole at Sawmill Falls. In another 0.2 mile you'll reach an old log bridge on the right; cross it and bear left onto Opal Creek Trail. Follow it 1 mile along the Little North Santiam River to reach an overlook at Opal Pool. You'll hear it before you see it: a roar of water charging through a narrow rock chasm before landing in a deep, clear-green pool. Return as you came, or follow the trail another 0.5 mile to a second log footbridge (slippery when wet) crossing Opal Creek and continuing up the creek into Opal Creek Wilderness.

Alternately, from the first footbridge off the main road trail, continue on the road 1 mile to Jawbone Flats, a circa-1929 mining camp that's been put to new use as an old-growth study center.

24 PAMELIA LAKE

Type ▪	Day hike or backpack
Difficulty ▪	Moderate for children
Distance ▪	4.4 miles round trip
Terrain ▪	Gentle ascent (800 feet elevation gain)
High point ▪	3920 feet
Hikable ▪	June through October
FYI ▪	Limited-entry permit required Memorial Day weekend to October 31
Contact ▪	Detroit Ranger District, (541) 854-3366

The trail to Pamelia Lake, in Mount Jefferson Wilderness, follows a lovely creek slipping through a venerable old-growth forest and ends at a large mountain lake. The lake's level drops over the summer, and the lake is most attractive from early July, when rhododendrons bloom, through August, though less crowded in September. Before making plans to go to Pamelia Lake, pick up limited-entry permits from the Detroit Ranger Station, in the town of Detroit off State Highway 22 (free at this writing, though a trailhead fee may also be required).

 From Detroit drive 12.5 miles south on State Highway 22 and turn east on Pamelia Road (Forest Road 2246). Follow the road 3.8 miles to the trailhead at the road's end (last 0.9 mile is gravel).

The trail begins as a wide, gently ascending path through the forest. A few minutes from the trailhead a sign indicates that you're entering Mount Jefferson Wilderness. Continue walking alongside rushing Pamelia Creek, lined with moss-draped, round rocks. The scene doesn't change much until about 1.9 miles, when something seems

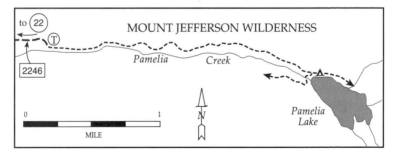

Pamelia Lake

different—the creek is gone! It's still within earshot at first, but over the final 0.3 mile to the lake it fades from hearing as well, and all you'll hear are bird calls and your own footfalls. Just beyond a trail junction at 2.2 miles lies Pamelia Lake. Camp only in designated sites.

25 MARION LAKE

Type ▪	Day hike or backpack
Difficulty ▪	Moderate for children
Distance ▪	5.4 miles, loop
Terrain ▪	Rolling or gently ascending (510 feet elevation gain)
High point ▪	4170 feet
Hikable ▪	June through September
Contact ▪	Detroit Ranger District, (503) 854-3366

An exceptionally beautiful lake and an interesting route getting there are what make this hike so appealing. Overnight camping at Marion

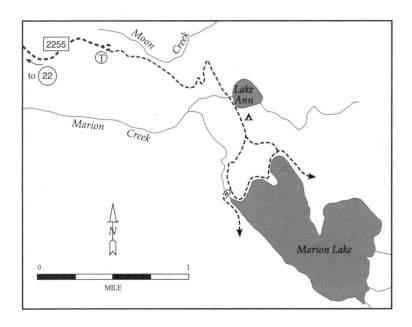

Lake is limited, though there are some nice campsites at Lake Ann, along the way. Camp only in designated sites.

 From Detroit drive south on State Highway 22 for 16.6 miles and turn left onto Forest Road 2255 (gravel after 0.7 mile). Continue 4.6 miles to the trailhead at the end of the road.

The wide trail follows a rolling, uphill grade most of the way. At about 0.4 mile the sound of Moon Creek can be heard, off to the left but out of sight. By 0.8 mile the sound has gone, replaced by the gurgle of little nearby springs. At about 1 mile the trail becomes steeper. Step across a small creek, then at 1.5 miles meet Lake Ann's outlet creek. Walk a short distance through a corridor of vine maple (brilliant in late September) and cross a jumble of rocks at the end of the lake; listen to the creek rumbling and singing underfoot.

Lake Ann is lovely, but its banks are either steep or marshy, not appealing for picnicking. Continue up the trail along the lakeshore, passing campsites at the lake's east end. A junction at 1.8 miles signals the start of the loop trail at Marion Lake's north end. Going clockwise, pass a scree slope and reach the lake and another trail fork in 0.3 mile. Bearing right, walk along a well-trampled slope above the lake until the trail resumes in about 0.2 mile, following around and above the lake. The trail switches back once to ascend a peninsula, then

Marion Lake

drops down to a gorgeous, substantial footbridge across the lake's outlet 1 mile from the start of the loop. Rather than cross the footbridge, bear right down the trail above the outlet creek that drops down to the start of the loop in 0.8 mile. From there, bear left and continue back to the trailhead on the main trail.

26 IRON MOUNTAIN

Type ▪ Day hike
Difficulty ▪ Moderate to strenuous for children
Distance ▪ 3.6 miles round trip
Terrain ▪ Steady, steep ascent (1385 feet elevation gain)
High point ▪ 5455 feet
Hikable ▪ June through October
Contact ▪ Sweet Home Ranger District, (541) 367-5168

The trail up Iron Mountain would seem a tougher climb if it weren't surrounded by a blaze of wildflowers at every step and if the goal weren't to reach an operating fire lookout. Still, this is a challenging hike, going straight up the mountain. It's also a favorite July wild-flower trek among many Oregon hikers. No camping is allowed.

From the junction of US Highway 20 and State Highway 126, head west on US 20 for 9 miles and turn south on Forest Road 15 to a small trailhead sign (at milepost 63). Continue 0.2 mile to a large parking area.

From the parking area, the trail cuts back through the woods, crosses the highway at 0.2 mile, and begins its climb with a gentle ascent through a deep, airy forest of old-growth Douglas fir. At about

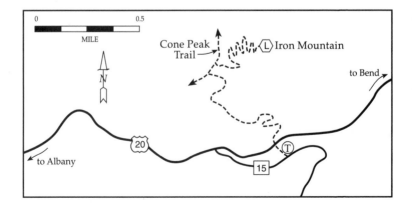

Mount Jefferson from Iron Mountain

0.8 mile the forest starts to open up, and at 1 mile the trail reaches a junction; bear right. In another 0.2 mile bear right again at the junction with Cone Peak Trail.

From the last junction, the trail is exposed (hot in summer) and quite steep. The consolation is the open fields of wildflowers blooming profusely in midsummer. Take time with children on this last 0.7 mile to the lookout, snooping at the flowers and enjoying the view opening up as the trail ascends. The summit isn't much more than a rocky knob without room for more than a lookout. Watch children carefully up here; it's safe enough if they don't start clambering down the rocks. Walk around the catwalk to take in the view of Mount Hood, Mount Jefferson, Mount Washington, the Three Sisters, and the tiptop of Three-Fingered Jack. Encourage children to sign the hikers' register; they may enjoy leafing through it to scan the hometowns of hikers that preceded them. Return as you came.

27 SAND MOUNTAIN

Type ■	Day hike
Difficulty ■	Easy for children
Distance ■	1.25 miles, loop
Terrain ■	Short, steep ascent (340 feet elevation gain)
High point ■	5459 feet
Hikable ■	June through October
Contact ■	McKenzie Ranger District, (541) 822-3381

The hike around the rim of the crater is just one part of what's sure to be a memorable family outing to Sand Mountain, located southwest of Hoodoo Ski Bowl. This cinder cone is the centerpiece of the Sand Mountain Geologic Special Interest Area, which was established in the late 1980s to protect it and neighboring cinder cones from off-road vehicle damage. But what children probably will find most interesting is the lookout cabin on the crater rim. Though it appears to have been there for years, it's actually a reconstructed cabin from Whiskey Peak in southern Oregon. It was reassembled (with

Sand Mountain Lookout

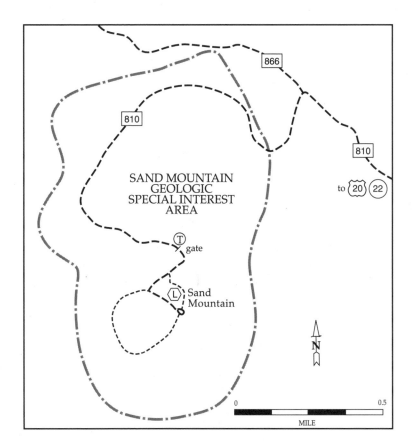

windows from another lookout and a fire-finder from yet another)
on the rim in 1989 and 1990. At last report, visitors were welcome on
the catwalk and inside to look through the fire-finder and talk with
the ranger about life on Sand Mountain.

From the junction of State Highway 22 and US Highway 20/State
Highway 126, drive east on US 20/State 22 for 5.5 miles and turn
south at the sign to Hoodoo Ski Bowl (Forest Road 2690). Continue
3.2 miles, following signs to Big Lake, and bear right onto dirt Forest Road 810. From here the dirt road is rocky and rutted in places,
but it's passable for slow-going passenger cars in summer.
Routefinding for the next 4.4 miles to the trailhead is a bit tricky,
however. After reaching a primitive horse camp in 0.7 mile, bear left
with the main road. At 1.5 miles bear left (should be signed). At 2.4 miles
go straight through a four-way junction. Take a sharp left at 2.9 miles
and continue another 1.5 miles to where the road ends at the gate.

Park and walk past the gate and up the road 0.1 mile, then veer left off the road onto a footpath. It's a steep, short route to the lookout at the summit of Sand Mountain, at 0.3 mile. Plan to spend some time visiting with the ranger and admiring the views—on very clear days—of Hoodoo Ski Bowl, Black Butte, Big Lake, Mount Washington, the Three Sisters, and Mount Hood.

To continue the hike, walk down the barren, sandy summit to the fenced turnaround at the end of the road and cross it through narrow openings in the fence. The trail drops down, steeply at first, to circumnavigate the crater. The rim trail isn't narrow enough to be dangerous, but the view is awesome, to the right into the small, steep-walled crater and to the left down the outside of the cinder cone. The trail levels out then climbs rather steeply before meeting the road. Follow the road back down past the gate to your car.

28 FRENCH PETE CREEK

Type ■	Day hike
Difficulty ■	Moderate for children
Distance ■	3.5 miles or more, round trip
Terrain ■	Gradual ascent (400 feet elevation gain)
High point ■	2200 feet
Hikable ■	Most of the year
Contact ■	Blue River Ranger District, (541) 822-3317

The low-elevation valley carved by French Pete Creek—supposedly named for an early-day sheepherder who roamed this country—offers

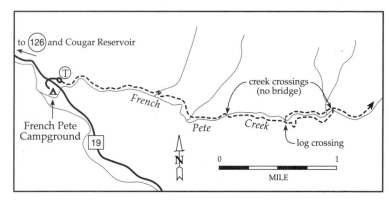

French Pete Creek

easy hiking in Three Sisters Wilderness through some wonderful old growth. Fall here is grand, with the yellow leaves of big-leaf maple pirouetting down to the creek. Bridges used to cross the creek at the 1.75- and 3-mile points; now, to go higher than 1.75 miles, you may need to wade. Camping is not allowed within 100 feet of the creek.

From Springfield follow State Highway 126 east 45 miles and turn right at the sign to Cougar Reservoir (Forest Road 19). At the fork veer right toward the reservoir and continue on Forest Road 19 another 10 miles. The trailhead is 1 mile past the end of the reservoir on the left, across the road from French Pete Campground.

The trail climbs steeply in places, following the north bank of the creek. It crosses a side creek at 0.9 mile and for the most part stays well above the creek, with spur trails leading down to several appealing creekside picnic sites. At 1.75 miles the trail meets the creek at the site of a former footbridge. When we last visited (spring 1999) one log remained of that bridge—not a safe crossing for children. It may be possible to walk downstream a bit and wade the creek in summer. If so, you can continue up the trail another 1.25 miles to a second creek crossing (again, no bridge, so wading is necessary). Alternately, with older children, recross the creek on a fallen log 0.5 mile above the site of the first footbridge; from here the trail continues for miles into the wilderness.

29 TAMOLITCH POOL

Type ▪ Day hike
Difficulty ▪ Moderate for children
Distance ▪ 4.6 miles round trip
Terrain ▪ Gradual ascent (200 feet elevation gain)
High point ▪ 2400 feet
Hikable ▪ Most of the year
Contact ▪ McKenzie Ranger District, (541) 822-3381

The McKenzie River Trail offers a lot of opportunities for hikes, including one-way treks with a shuttle car. It runs 26.5 miles from McKenzie Bridge north to Fish Lake, with about ten access points along the way—and ten areas to choose from for day hikes. The 2.3-mile hike from Trailbridge Reservoir to Tamolitch Pool is one good choice. It's uncrowded and low enough in elevation to be accessible most of the year, and it follows close to the river most of the way. Although fairly uneventful, the walk to the pool ends with a view of deep, round, turquoise Tamolitch Pool, and a mystery: Where does the water come from? (Keep reading.)

To reach the upper trailhead from McKenzie Bridge east of Springfield, take State Highway 126 north about 15 miles and turn west onto Forest Road 730 at the sign to Trailbridge Reservoir. After crossing the river, bear right up gravel Forest Road 612 and drive 0.5 mile to a bend in the road, where you'll see the trailhead sign and enough parking for a few cars.

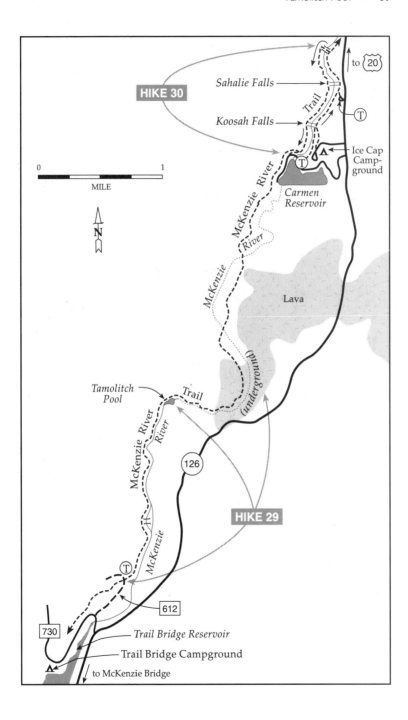

HIKE 30

Sahalie Falls

Koosah Falls

to 20

Trail

T

Ice Cap
Campground

Carmen
Reservoir

McKenzie River

River

0   1
MILE

N

Lava

McKenzie

Tamolitch
Pool

Trail

(underground)

McKenzie River

River

126

HIKE 29

McKenzie

T

612

730

Trail Bridge Reservoir

Trail Bridge Campground

to McKenzie Bridge

Tamolitch Pool

The trail is fairly level for the first 1.5 miles or so. The McKenzie River is placid and within view much of the way. Cross a footbridge over a side creek after about 1 mile. About halfway to Tamolitch Pool the river picks up steam, tumbling and churning, as the trail gets a little steeper. You'll know you're getting close to Tamolitch Pool when a lot of old lava rock appears on either side of the trail, even underfoot. The trail stays above the river, granting occasional views down to the rushing water. Then, suddenly, the rushing stops, and you'll be looking down into clear Tamolitch Pool from atop a rock cliff. A sign calls it Tamolitch Falls, and it's easy to imagine the dramatic waterfall that would tumble down the sheer cliff at the far end of the pool if flows were high enough. Instead, the water seeps in invisibly. Above the pond, the river disappears into porous lava rock underground as far upstream as Carmen Reservoir. (Some flow would probably be seen on the surface if much of the river weren't also diverted from Carmen to Smith Reservoir, reentering the McKenzie below Tamolitch.) Explore, looking for tree molds left years ago when flowing lava surrounded standing trees. Return as you came.

With a shuttle car, Tamolitch Pool could serve as a stop on a one-way, downhill hike 5.2 miles from Carmen Reservoir to Trailbridge Reservoir.

30 SAHALIE FALLS–KOOSAH FALLS

Type ▪	Day hike
Difficulty ▪	Moderate for children
Distance ▪	4 miles, loop
Terrain ▪	Gradual ascent (400 feet elevation gain)
High point ▪	3000 feet
Hikable ▪	April through November
Contact ▪	McKenzie Ranger District, (541) 822-3381

Koosah Falls and, especially, Sahalie Falls are popular stopping points along the McKenzie River Highway. Trails on either side of the rushing river enable hikers to make a 4-mile loop that takes in both falls from both sides. The forest is lush, with tall trees, and the terrain is gentle. Kids will enjoy getting to see the two dramatic falls twice, plus crossing the McKenzie River on a high, narrow, log footbridge.

You can start the hike at several points; the simplest is the Sahalie Falls viewpoint. From McKenzie Bridge take State Highway 126 north about 22 miles to the turnout at Sahalie Falls, on the west side of the road.

To hike counterclockwise, walk upriver (north), pausing to admire the falls from developed viewpoints along the way. Continue along the path 0.5 mile to its junction with the McKenzie River Trail. A right turn leads toward State 126 and Clear Lake; instead, turn left to cross a narrow footbridge over the river.

The trail rolls downstream through old-growth trees and past a small outcrop of lava, leading back past Sahalie Falls, the foam at its base turning turquoise in sunlight. Continue down the trail, passing Koosah Falls about 0.7 mile past Sahalie. At about 2.5 miles bear left at a trail junction, leaving the McKenzie River Trail on a short spur leading to Carmen Reservoir.

Koosah Falls

The trail ends at the road around the reservoir. Follow the road to the left, across the McKenzie, then immediately look for a trail heading up the other side of the river. The trail up the east bank follows the river more closely. About 0.2 mile from the reservoir, pass a spur trail to Ice Cap Campground, then in another 0.2 mile arrive at a viewpoint overlooking Koosah Falls. Look for the springs gushing out of rocks at the base of the falls. The trail continues as a path and occasional stairs until it merges with the viewpoint trails at Sahalie Falls.

３１ CLEAR LAKE

Type ▪ Day hike
Difficulty ▪ Moderate for children
Distance ▪ 5 miles, loop
Terrain ▪ Nearly level
High point ▪ 3040 feet
Hikable ▪ April through October
Contact ▪ McKenzie Ranger District, (541) 822-3381

Clear Lake is an exquisitely pure lake high in the mountains and just off State Highway 126. The level trail that encircles the lake will interest children every step of the way: it passes through magnificent old-growth forest, winds along the sunny lakeshore, fords the McKenzie River on a log footbridge, and crosses over an extensive lava flow. On the lake's west side, the hike follows a portion of the McKenzie River Trail. Along the lakeshore the route passes a campground and a picnic area as well as a rustic resort that rents rowboats by the hour. No motorboats are allowed on Clear Lake, thus preserving its purity and tranquility for hikers and boaters alike. Wear sturdy boots; ankle-twisting lava rocks are sharp through thin soles.

From McKenzie Bridge drive north on State Highway 126 about 23 miles and turn right at the sign to Coldwater Cove Campground. Follow the road around to the boat ramp at the end of the campground and park in the parking area. You can also start the hike at the resort and picnic area on the other side of the lake. But starting a counterclockwise hike from Coldwater Cove gets kids onto the intriguing lava flow quickly and gets the hottest part of the hike over with while they're fresh.

Head north on the McKenzie River Trail through big trees, passing a lot of anglers' spur trails to the lake. Soon the dirt-surface trail turns to asphalt when it reaches the lava flow. The vine maple here turns color sooner than in the forest, due to the stress of living with little water and among hot rocks. Continue across the lava for about 0.4 mile.

Enter the forest, then reemerge onto another 0.4-mile-wide lava flow. Reenter the woods and shortly pass a clear, blue-green cove— the site of Great Springs, one of the largest of several springs that

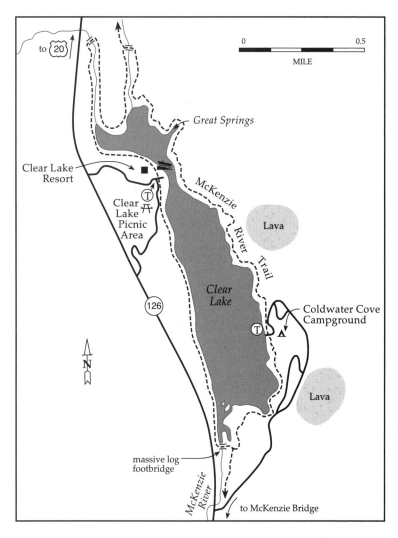

feed Clear Lake. At 1.8 miles cross a stream bed on a footbridge. At the end of the bridge, at a trail junction, the McKenzie River Trail heads to the right; bear left instead, heading around the north end of the lake. At a trail-side bench there's a good view south to the Three Sisters. Following an inlet creek, the trail approaches the highway, then crosses the creek and heads back toward the lake. Clear Lake Resort is at about 3 miles; continue a short distance past the resort cabins and store and up the paved road. Leave the road near the picnic area's rest rooms, where the trail resumes. Cross a small, musical

Clear Lake

creek, then cross the lake's outlet—the McKenzie River—on a massive footbridge at 4.1 miles. In 0.1 mile you'll again meet the McKenzie River Trail; follow it to the left 0.8 mile more, along the lakeshore and across a lava flow, to find yourself back at the parking area.

32 PROXY FALLS

Type ■	Day hike
Difficulty ■	Easy for children
Distance ■	1.25 miles, loop
Terrain ■	Level after slight ascent
High point ■	3200 feet
Hikable ■	Late June through October
Contact ■	McKenzie Ranger District, (541) 822-3381

For a short hike to two spectacular waterfalls, choose this trail. The highway leading to the trailhead closes in winter; shortly after it opens, the rhododendrons and bear grass start blooming along the trail. A hike to Proxy Falls is a great way to break up a trip between Eugene and Sisters.

Proxy Falls Trail

From the junction of State Highways 126 and 242, take State 242 (the old McKenzie Highway scenic route, which is closed in winter) east 9 miles to the trailhead, marked with signs and a substantial rest room on the left.

The trail starts across the road from the rest rooms. It's now a loop route, with signs directing hikers one way (presumably to reduce encounters with other hikers on this popular trail). Immediately head up, crossing an ancient lava flow. A spur to the right leads to Lower Proxy Falls, where Proxy Creek slides 200 feet down a curved cliff face, as if outlining a vase. In another 0.25 mile there's a second spur, to Upper Proxy Falls. Here water from springs high above fall more than 100 feet over a stair-step cliff thick with velvety moss. The placid pool at the base is inviting for toe dipping. Back on the main trail, continue 0.3 mile, crossing a little footbridge and that same lava flow, to return to the trailhead just east of where you started.

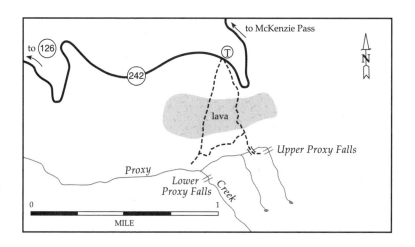

33 LINTON LAKE

Type ▪ Day hike or backpack
Difficulty ▪ Moderate for children
Distance ▪ 3.8 miles round trip
Terrain ▪ Gentle or briefly steep ascent (300 feet elevation gain)
High point ▪ 3550 feet
Hikable ▪ Late June through November
Contact ▪ McKenzie Ranger District, (541) 822-3381

Trailhead parking for Linton Lake can be tight in midsummer—for good reason. It's a very gentle ascent to this stunning, deep green lake that feels more remote, more distant from civilization, than it is in miles.

From the junction of State Highways 126 and 242, take State 242 (the old McKenzie Highway scenic route, which is closed in winter) east 10.5 miles to a trailhead parking area on the left at Alder Springs Campground, just before milepost 66. The trail starts across the road.

Slowly descend through Douglas fir forest, climb a few switchbacks, cross a stream bed, then drop over a vine maple-covered ridge at 1 mile. More switchbacks drop to where the trail levels and grants hikers their first view of the lake at 1.4 miles. Continue

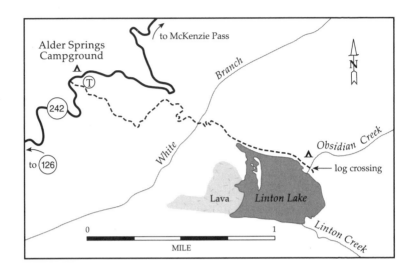

another 0.5 mile to where the trail dips to the lake near some campsites by Obsidian Creek. Cross the creek on a big log and follow an informal trail through the willows to a sandy beach jutting into the lake—a wonderfully serene, scenic spot. Return as you came.

Linton Lake

34 BENSON LAKE

Type ▪ Day hike
Difficulty ▪ Moderate for children
Distance ▪ 2.8 miles, round trip
Terrain ▪ Steady ascent (370 feet elevation gain)
High point ▪ 5190 feet
Hikable ▪ July through October
Contact ▪ McKenzie Ranger District, (541) 822-3381

From the junction of State Highways 126 and 242, take State 242 (the old McKenzie Highway scenic route, which is closed in winter) east 16 miles and turn left at the sign to Scott Lake. Continue 1.5 miles on the gravel road along the lake, bearing left at the sign to Benson Trailhead, to the parking area at road's end.

The trail climbs steadily, bordered by huckleberries and purple lousewort (a much prettier wildflower than the name implies) and shaded by alpine fir. There are no noteworthy landmarks until you catch a glimpse of the blue lake off to your left; an informal trail leads to a toe-dipping spot. Informal trails lead you part way around the lake in either direction. (The main trail continues, reaching a spur to the Tenas Lakes in another mile.) Return as you came.

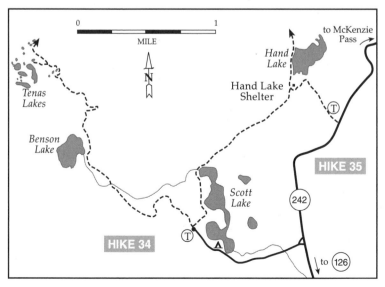

Benson Lake

35 HAND LAKE

Type ■	Day hike or backpack
Difficulty ■	Easy for children
Distance ■	1 mile round trip
Terrain ■	Nearly level
High point ■	4750 feet
Hikable ■	July through October
Contact ■	McKenzie Ranger District, (541) 822-3381

The short hike to Hand Lake will suit some young members of your party just fine. The lake sits in a broad meadow, golden in late summer, the kind of place that invites a long snooze in the grass. More energetic hikers could walk another 1.5 miles across the meadow and around the end of Scott Lake to the campground road.

From the junction of State Highways 126 and 242, take State 242 (the old McKenzie Highway scenic route, which is closed in winter) east 17 miles (1 mile past the road to Scott Lake) to a small trailhead parking turnout.

The trail heads northwest into the woods, climbing ever so slightly to reach three-sided Hand Lake Shelter at 0.5 mile. The lake lies before you, 0.25 mile to the north—not much more than a muddy handprint in late summer, bordered on the north by a lava flow. Explore the muddy shore, watching for tracks—deer, birds, Reebok, Vibram—and looking for tiny frogs the exact color of mud. The trail continues north along the lava flow or south to Scott Lake, unless you've arranged a pick-up at the Scott Lake trailhead (shared with Benson Lake; see Hike 34).

Hand Lake Shelter

36 LITTLE BELKNAP CRATER

Type	▪ Day hike
Difficulty	▪ Strenuous for children
Distance	▪ 5.2 miles round trip
Terrain	▪ Steady ascent on sharp lava (1100 feet)
High point	▪ 6305 feet
Hikable	▪ July through October
Contact	▪ McKenzie Ranger District, (541) 822-3381

It's a hike like no other, crossing a huge lava flow most of the way. Wear boots; you'll shred your sneakers on the sharp rock. Is this a good kids' hike? I wasn't sure until I asked a couple of kids, ages eight and ten, halfway to the summit. Their response: all smiles, two thumbs up. "But not a first hike," they cautioned, and their parents nodded. Later, on the summit, I met three more children, ranging from six to twelve years old. Tough, but not too tough for motivated kids.

 From the junction of State Highways 126 and 242, take State 242 (the old McKenzie Highway scenic route, which is closed in winter) about 22 miles nearly to McKenzie Pass. The trailhead is on the north side of the highway, about 0.5 mile west of rock-walled Dee

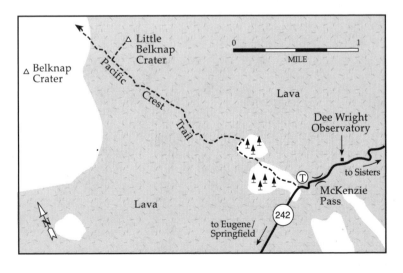

North and Middle Sister from Little Belknap Crater Trail

Wright Observatory. Coming from Sisters, travel on State 242 west about 15 miles.

The route follows the Pacific Crest Trail north toward Mount Washington. It's not steep (except at the very end), but it's steadily up, with loose, rough lava stones underfoot most of the way. The trail begins in the forest, crosses a narrow band of lava, and returns to the trees for 0.3 mile more, following just inside the edge of a forested rise. (A lot of ripe huckleberries grow here in late summer). At 0.75 mile the trail makes a sharp left turn and the real hike begins, with nothing but lava from here to the summit. At 2.3 miles turn right on the spur trail to the summit. The final few steps to the top begin with a walk and end with a scramble. From the summit, survey the gray-black sea of lava that surrounds your perch, with red Belknap Crater rising smoothly to the west and snowcapped North and Middle Sister to the south. Return as you came.

37 MARYS PEAK

Type ▪ Day hike
Hikable ▪ April through November
Contact ▪ Waldport Ranger District,
(541) 563-3211

SUMMIT

Difficulty ▪ Easy for children
Distance ▪ 1.4 miles round trip
Terrain ▪ Steady ascent (337 feet elevation gain)
High point ▪ 4097 feet

MEADOWEDGE TRAIL LOOP

Difficulty ▪ Easy for children
Distance ▪ 2 miles, loop
Terrain ▪ Steady ascent (480 feet elevation gain)
High point ▪ 3880 feet

NORTH RIDGE TRAIL LOOP

Difficulty ▪ Moderate for children
Distance ▪ 3.5 miles, loop
Terrain ▪ Rolling or steady ascent (660 feet)
High point ▪ 3800 feet

For a young child new to hiking, the 0.7-mile trek to the top of Marys Peak is a great adventure (even if it is on a gravel road). As the highest peak in the Coast Range, Marys Peak, to a child, can feel like the top of the world. Older children may enjoy the longer, woodsier North Ridge Trail Loop; all ages will enjoy the Meadowedge Trail Loop. Other hikes are also possible, including one-way hikes with a shuttle car (see map). Summer is the best season here, with penstemon, Columbia lilies, lupine, and other wildflowers festooning the upper slopes. Think of Marys Peak during shoulder seasons as well, when clouds sometimes swirl eerily among the noble firs and around the treeless summit.

 From US Highway 20 in Philomath, west of Corvallis, turn south onto State Highway 34 and drive 9 miles to Marys Peak Road (FR 3010); turn right. Drive 10 miles to the gate at the summit parking lot.

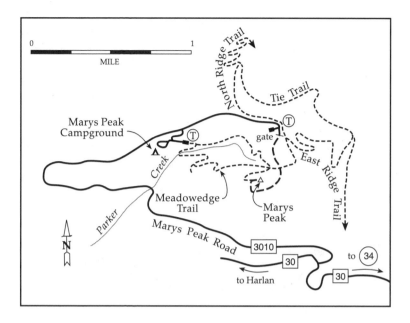

SUMMIT

Walk the gravel road leading up (barred to all but utility vehicles serving the transmission towers on the summit). The route is mostly above tree line, though you'll pass through stands of Douglas fir and noble fir; can you tell the difference? Cones at the base of the trees provide clues. Though relatively low by Cascade standards, Marys Peak is the highest point for thousands of miles from the west and for more than 50 miles from the east. Consequently, it can be windy on top. No place on a mountain summit is really sheltered, but wander around to find the least windy site for a picnic. A footpath also leads to the summit (see map).

MEADOWEDGE TRAIL LOOP

This trail was constructed with young hikers in mind. It passes in and out of woods and meadows, keeping things interesting and varied. From the gate at the main trailhead, take the summit road trail 0.2 mile to the signed start of Meadowedge Trail on the right. (Alternately, follow a spur trail up from the picnic area at Marys Peak Campground.) Walk the narrow path through the grassy meadow about 30 yards and enter a deep forest, where there is a trailhead sign and map. To walk the 1.6-mile loop clockwise, go straight at the first

Crossing Parker Creek on Meadowedge Trail

trail junction. For the first few minutes you'll be walking just inside the forest's edge, until the trail enters a wildflower-strewn meadow. It loops back into the woods, which offer their own summer bouquet of bleeding hearts and oxalis. Wind down through the airy old-growth forest to a little bridge crossing Parker Creek, marking the loop's halfway point. Just beyond is the spur to the campground, on the left. The main trail climbs just inside the forest until it completes the loop; bear left to return to the summit trail.

NORTH RIDGE TRAIL LOOP

Construction of the Tie Trail linking the East and North Ridge Trails created a meditative, moderately graded, woodsy loop on Marys Peak. From the summit parking area, pick up the North Ridge Trail heading north, descending gently. After a couple of switchbacks, watch for a junction (easy to miss) with the Tie Trail, on the right at 0.7 mile. Follow it as it rolls along to the south to a more obvious junction with the East Ridge Trail at 1.8 miles. Bear right and climb the hillside switchbacks; at 3.1 miles the trail merges with a footpath leading down from the summit. Follow it back to the parking area.

38 WOODPECKER LOOP

Type ▪ Day hike
Difficulty ▪ Easy for children
Distance ▪ 1.2 miles, loop
Terrain ▪ Gradual ascent (300 feet elevation gain)
Hikable ▪ Year-round
High point ▪ 420 feet
Contact ▪ William L. Finley National Wildlife Refuge, (541) 757-7236

Finley Refuge is one in a chain of three Willamette Valley refuges designated to provide winter habitat for Canada geese, including the dusky Canada goose, whose numbers have been dwindling. The best time to visit the refuge is October through March, when there are sure to be plenty of geese. This loop trail winds through a variety of habitats typical of this transition zone between the Coast Range and the Willamette Valley. It's the only trail in the refuge that's open through the winter; the others close to avoid disturbing the geese. Watch for poison oak.

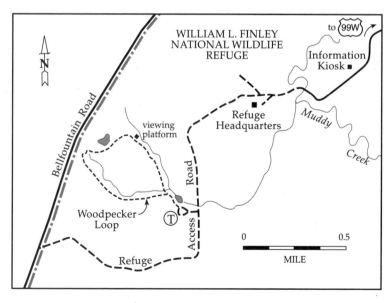

From Corvallis, take US Highway 99W south 10 miles and turn west at the sign to Finley Refuge. After 1.3 miles turn south and drive 2.3 miles to the signed trailhead for Woodpecker Loop, passing rest rooms and an information kiosk at 0.8 mile.

Follow the trail past a signboard and pond, where the frog- and newt-catchers in the party can have a field day. Just 0.1 mile from the trailhead, the trail splits to start the loop. Bearing right, the trail reaches a huge oak encircled by a wooden viewing platform at 0.3 mile; it looks out over a dry, grassy hillside scattered with more native oaks. Interpretive signs offer information about the area's ecology.

Continuing on, the nearly level trail winds mostly through a mixed forest of big-leaf maple, Douglas fir, and Oregon white oak, dipping also into ash swales and dense stands of second-growth Douglas fir. Listen and look for five different kinds of woodpeckers along the way.

Birdwatching off Woodpecker Loop

39 MOUNT PISGAH

Type ▪ Day hike
Hikable ▪ Year-round
Contact ▪ Lane County Parks, (541) 682-6940, or
Mount Pisgah Arboretum, (541) 747-3817

SUMMIT
Difficulty ▪ Moderate to strenuous for children
Distance ▪ 2.8 to 3 miles round trip
Terrain ▪ Steady to steep ascent (1046 feet
elevation gain)
High point ▪ 1516 feet

WATER GARDEN
Difficulty ▪ Easy for children
Distance ▪ 1 mile round trip
Terrain ▪ Nearly level
High point ▪ 470 feet

Above you, a red-tailed hawk rides an updraft, eventually gliding out of sight behind the oak-mantled hill. Below, the silver ribbon of the Willamette River's Coast Fork unfurls along the mountain's base, bordering a patchwork of small farms: pumpkins, mint, you-cut flowers.

For most visitors to Howard Buford Recreation Area, minutes from Eugene, the heart-pumping hike to the summit of Mount Pisgah is the number-one destination. Certainly plenty of kids make the trek. Stick to the wider main trails to avoid coming in contact with the ever-present poison oak. With younger children, consider an outing on the shorter, more level trails in Mount Pisgah Arboretum, at the mountain's base; maps at the trailhead outline the many options, with paths leading to river or pond or creek or wildflower garden. Here are two popular choices: one challenging and one easy.

From I-5 at the south end of Eugene/Springfield, take exit 189 (or take 30th Avenue South from Eugene) and follow signs 2.5 miles across the Coast Fork Willamette River. Bear right to reach the west trailhead and main parking area, or bear left to reach the north trailhead and horse arena.

SUMMIT

Most summit hikers take the West Summit Trail, which begins at the west trailhead, adjacent to the main parking area at the end of the road. From the trailhead, wind up through grassy meadows and in and out of oak groves on a broad—though sometimes rocky—trail. At 0.6 mile the trail reaches a junction with Bridge Bowl Trail—a good spot to stop and enjoy the view to the west of the Coast Fork and across the lower Willamette Valley to Spencer Butte. (Just ahead on the right is what we used to call the "backpack tree"; when the kids were little, we'd have them hike this far before we'd put them in baby backpacks and carry them the rest of the way.)

Unlike many summit trails, this one grows less steep the higher it ascends. At 1.4 miles it emerges from a grove of oaks onto the grassy, treeless summit. You'll want to linger here over the bronze sighting pedestal, commissioned by noted writer Ken Kesey and his wife Faye and installed at the summit in 1990. On top there's a relief map of the surrounding territory; on the sides, bas-relief depictions of leaves and seeds, shells, animals, birds, fish, and other evidence of life forms that have dwelt in Oregon over the past 200 million years. Bring paper and crayons or pastels to make rubbings of your favorite critters, or settle for a game of "I Spy": an octopus, a leaf, a map of the world, a winged maple seed. Return as you came.

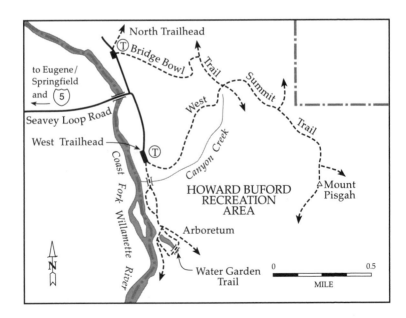

Sighting pedestal atop Mount Pisgah

For an alternate route to the summit, after crossing the river and entering the park, turn left (toward the horse arena) and park at the north trailhead. From here the Bridge Bowl Trail leads up and across the grassy hillside to meet the West Summit Trail at 0.8 mile; all together it's a little less steep and just a little longer than the West Summit route.

WATER GARDEN

The route to the pond area known as the Water Garden leads through a wildflower garden, alongside the river, and to a long pond with a high bridge from which you might spot turtles, if you're lucky. Drive to the main parking area and walk south, into the arboretum. Follow the wide Quarry Road Trail or swing right onto McCall Riverbank Trail, site of the wildflower garden. Shortly after the two trails meet again bear right, then quickly left, to swing clockwise through the Water Garden, crossing the pond on Adikson Bridge. Loop back on one of several paths to the Quarry Road to return. A river beach near the start of the Water Garden loop is appealing in summer.

For more fun exploring: Allow time to pick your own produce on the way home; just outside the park, several farms along Seavey Loop Road offer berries, flowers, pumpkins, and more, depending upon the season.

40 SPENCER BUTTE

Type ▪	Day hike
Difficulty ▪	Moderate to strenuous for children
Distance ▪	1 to 3 miles, round trip
Terrain ▪	Steady to steep ascent (770 feet elevation gain)
High point ▪	2052 feet
Hikable ▪	Year-round
Contact ▪	Eugene Parks, Recreation and Cultural Services, (541) 687-5333

Forested Spencer Butte dominates Eugene's southern skyline, signaling the end of the Willamette Valley and the beginning of hilly southern Oregon. Like Mount Pisgah (Hike 39), it's a wonderful, close-in summit hike for kids willing to do some trudging for a top-of-the-world view, and there's plenty of poison oak. Unlike Mount

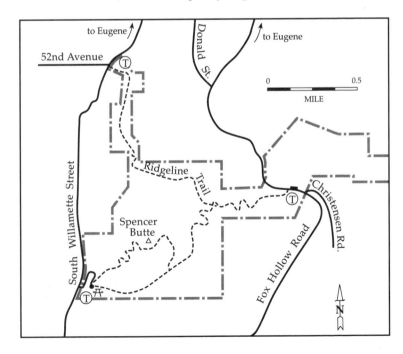

Snacking alongside Spencer Butte Trail

Pisgah, you'll be hiking in deep forest with no big views until the big payoff at the summit.

From the center of Eugene, follow South Willamette Street south to the entrance to Spencer Butte Park, on the east side of the street about 1 mile before its junction with Fox Hollow Road.

Steps lead out of the large parking area; bear left immediately to take the shorter, steeper route to the top (1 mile round trip). Much of this route is seemingly straight up, using steps and even requiring a little clambering to reach the rocky outcrop marking the summit. Alternately, from the steps at the parking area, go straight, following the wide path leading east and more slowly circling around the butte (3 miles round trip). The trail can be incredibly muddy in the rainy season, though a boardwalk crosses the worst spots. At 0.5 mile a spur trail from the Ridgeline Trail comes in from the right; stay on the main trail to where it degenerates into a tangle of trails just below the tree line. Do your best to stay on the main trail to avoid worsening the erosion here. If you're observant you can stay on some semblance of trail all the way to the summit outcrop; if not, you'll find yourself scrambling at the end.

For a longer summit hike, consider starting on the Ridgeline Trail at the Fox Hollow Road trailhead (4.8 miles round trip, 1090 feet elevation gain) or at the trailhead farther along on South Willamette Street, 0.75 mile north of the park entrance (5.8 miles round trip, 1090 feet elevation gain).

41 FALL CREEK

Type ▪ Day hike
Hikable ▪ Year-round
Contact ▪ Middle Fork Ranger District,
(541) 782-2283

LOWER SECTION
Difficulty ▪ Easy for children
Distance ▪ 3.5 miles one way
Terrain ▪ Rolling (120 feet elevation gain)
High point ▪ 1000 feet

LOWER MIDDLE SECTION
Difficulty ▪ Easy for children
Distance ▪ 1.7 miles one way
Terrain ▪ Rolling (80 feet elevation gain)
High point ▪ 1080 feet

UPPER MIDDLE SECTION
Difficulty ▪ Moderate for children
Distance ▪ 4.1 miles one way
Terrain ▪ Level, plus steady ascent (240 feet
elevation gain)
High point ▪ 1320 feet

UPPER SECTION
Difficulty ▪ Easy to moderate for children
Distance ▪ 4.7 miles one way
Terrain ▪ Gentle ascent (150 feet elevation gain)
High point ▪ 1300 feet

What makes Fall Creek Trail so appealing to families isn't any high drama; it's a pretty, low-key path along a low-elevation mountain

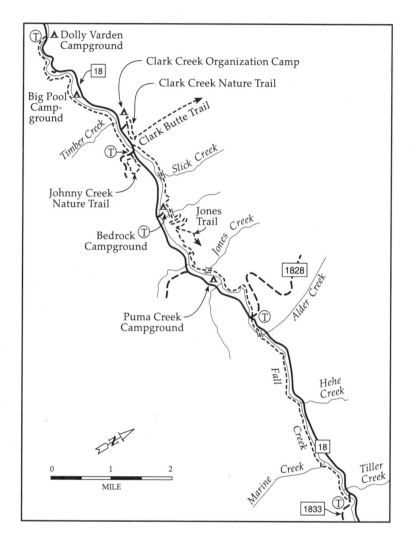

creek. Rather, it's the big trees; gorgeous, narrow canyon; sparkling, ice-cold stream; sprinkling of footbridges; and proximity to Eugene. It's grand in summer, when the goal may be to spend the day on a sunny stretch of beach. In winter the warming walk through deep forest is destination enough. The road meets the 14-mile-long trail at five points, naturally dividing the trail into four sections; make an out-and-back hike from any of the trailheads, or plan a one-way hike with shuttle car. There are potential campsites along the way, but this trail is more suitable for day hikes.

From Eugene take I-5 south to State Highway 58 and follow it 13 miles, exiting at the town of Lowell. From Lowell follow signs 3 miles north and turn right onto Fall Creek Road, just before the Unity covered bridge. Follow it 10 miles (it becomes Forest Road 18) to the end of the trail, across the road from Dolly Varden Campground.

LOWER SECTION

This trail stretches from Johnny Creek to Dolly Varden Campground. This is a fun section; but as the first section, it gets the most use, and the road is often in sight, albeit across the creek. Safest parking at the upper end is at the start of the Johnny Creek Nature Trail, just off Forest Road 18 on the right. Walk the short distance back to Forest Road 18, then head west following the gravel road on the creek's south bank.

It's a little confusing in here, with various side trails leading every which way. The simplest route: Follow the gravel road about 0.3 mile to an informal campground and pick up the trail that bears right, down toward the creek. At 0.5 mile the trail leads over a log bridge crossing Timber Creek. Back along Fall Creek the trail hugs the bank. Follow its ups and downs over three small footbridges. You'll know you're at about the 2-mile point when you see railing across the river indicating Big Pool Campground. The last 1.5 miles roll along next to the now-placid creek; you'll cross several more footbridges before hitting the lower trailhead at Dolly Varden Campground.

LOWER MIDDLE SECTION

You will follow this trail from Bedrock Campground to Johnny Creek. The high point of this short stretch is a wonderful swimming hole at Slick Creek. The upper trailhead is at Bedrock Campground, on the north side of Forest Road 18 about 4.5 miles east of Dolly Varden Campground. Drive into Bedrock Campground and follow the camping loop. At the far end of the loop, turn right into a large, signed trailhead parking area. Follow the trail through the trees, bearing right at a junction at 0.25 mile (a left turn loops back to the campground). The level trail now follows just above the creek. Rather treacherous little skid trails lead down to the creek at various points.

Fall Creek

Try to restrain the kids and wait until you reach a substantial foot-bridge over Slick Creek at about 0.6 mile; here you'll find easy access to good swimming and wading spots, a beach, and flat rocks for lazing around. At about the halfway point the trail starts climbing briefly, then drops. Cross creeks on two more footbridges before meeting the road at the start of Clark Butte Trail.

UPPER MIDDLE SECTION

This section, from Forest Road 1828 to Bedrock Campground, is the most remote of the four and the least level, with an elevation gain of more than 200 feet. The upper trailhead is on the north side of Forest Road 18 at the start of Forest Road 1828, 7 miles east of Dolly Varden Campground. The trail here is narrow but easy to follow and relatively level, and runs through a lovely forest of big trees alongside the exquisite creek. At 0.3 mile cross a side creek on a log bridge. At about 0.8 mile notice the fantastical rock formations on the stream; if kids are old enough, they will enjoy swimming here on a hot day. At about 1.3 miles the trail starts veering away from the creek and into a grove of magnificent old growth. Another 0.2 mile of hiking leads to a crest above the creek. The trail then drops slightly, crossing Jones Creek on a long log bridge. From there, the trail leads away from the creek again and begins a serious climb. The trail isn't steep, but the hillside is, and the trail gets a little rockier. At about 2.8 miles, after a couple of switchbacks, you'll reach the trail's crest at a little peeled-log bench with a view of a clear cut and, below it, a farm. The trail descends over the next 0.5 mile. At 3.3 miles, bear left at the junction with Jones Trail. Now the trail starts its real descent, switchbacking into a grove of rhododendrons. At the junction, a sign for Fall Creek Trail points to the right; follow it 0.25 mile and across pretty Bedrock Creek to the trailhead at Bedrock Campground.

UPPER SECTION

The upper end of the trail is just off Forest Road 18 on Forest Road 1833. (The trail stretches between Forest Road 1828 and Road 1833.) The trail stays close to the creek the entire way, traversing a gorgeous old-growth forest. For a short jaunt, start at the Road 1828 trailhead and hike as far as the footbridge, at 0.4 mile.

For more fun exploring: Consider a stroll along either of two nature loop trails: Clark Creek (1 mile) or Johnny Creek (0.75 mile, wheelchair accessible).

42 GOODMAN CREEK

Type ▪ Day hike or backpack
Difficulty ▪ Moderate for children
Distance ▪ 4 miles round trip
Terrain ▪ Gentle ascent (300 feet elevation gain)
High point ▪ 1150 feet
Hikable ▪ Year-round
Contact ▪ Middle Fork Ranger District,
(541) 782-2283

A gentle walk through stunning old-growth forest, leading to a footbridge across a lovely, wide stream: The hike to Goodman Creek is appealing year-round. In late winter you'll see plenty of newts crawling across the trail; later look for trilliums at trail side.

From Eugene take I-5 south to State Highway 58 and pull off at the wide trailhead parking area on the right, just west of milepost 21.

Just 0.2 mile from the trailhead you'll meet Goodman Creek Trail; bear right. The trail rounds an arm of Lookout Point Reservoir at some distance (a blessing, for it's not particularly scenic, especially at low winter water levels). At 1.9 miles there's a campsite and a spur leading left to a lovely waterfall and swimming hole. Continue on the

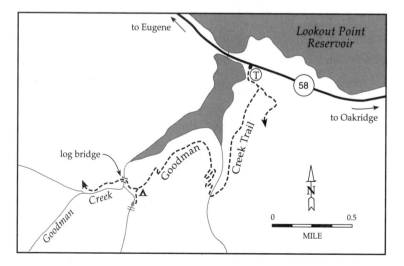

Goodman Creek

main trail another 0.1 mile to the long log footbridge crossing Goodman Creek. This is a great picnic spot and a good turnaround with children (though the trail continues). Return as you came.

43 SPIRIT AND MOON FALLS

Type ■ Day hike
Hikable ■ Most of the year
Contact ■ Cottage Grove Ranger District, (541) 942-5591

SPIRIT FALLS
Difficulty ■ Easy for children
Distance ■ 0.8 mile round trip
Terrain ■ Short, steep ascent (200 feet elevation gain)
High point ■ 2000 feet

MOON FALLS
Difficulty ■ Easy for children
Distance ■ 1.2 miles round trip
Terrain ■ Gentle ascent (100 feet elevation gain)
High point ■ 3100 feet

Hikes to either of these enchanting waterfalls are so short and so close together that you might as well visit both. The names are alluring enough, and they fulfill their promise of magic to hikers, especially

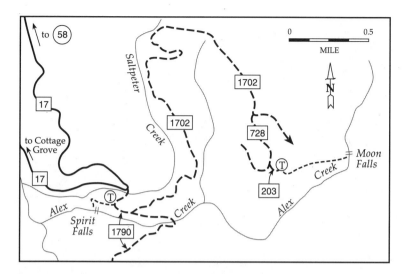

those visiting in spring, when stream flows are high, or in summer, when cooling mists from the falls are most welcome.

The quickest route from Eugene is via State Highway 58. Just past milepost 24, turn right up Patterson Mountain Road (Forest Road 5840), bearing right at the first Y. Follow this gravel road 9.7 miles up and over Patterson Saddle (where it becomes Forest Road 17) and down to Forest Road 1790; turn left onto Road 1790. Immediately to the right is a wide spot—the trailhead for Spirit Falls. To reach Moon Falls, drive 0.2 mile beyond the Spirit Falls trailhead on Forest Road 1790 and bear left on Forest Road 1702. Drive 2.8 miles and turn right on Forest Road 1702-728. Go 0.3 mile, bear left on Forest Road 1702-203, and continue 0.1 mile to the trailhead, where further progress by vehicles is blocked.

SPIRIT FALLS

The trail drops gently, levels somewhat, and then begins to drop rather steeply down a dirt path that's slippery when wet. It ends at the base of 60-foot Spirit Falls, which gushes over domed cliffs. There's a picnic table at a viewpoint overlooking the falls, and the pool at the base of the umbrellalike falls is small and inviting for wading (though swimming, per se, is prohibited in the Layng Creek watershed). Return as you came.

MOON FALLS

Begin walking along the overgrown spur road you drove in on. At about 0.3 mile the route turns into a narrow forest footpath. As you

Spirit Falls

hike in listen for the low booming of grouse. The trail ends at the base of the falls, which streams down a broad cliff in rivulets that run together before plunging into the pool below. Plan to linger a while at the falls, watching for water ouzels dipping in the stream, exploring the pool and Alex Creek, and perhaps picnicking at a table there. Return as you came.

ERMA BELL LAKES

Type ◼ Day hike or backpack
Difficulty ◼ Moderate for children
Distance ◼ 5.5 miles round trip
Terrain ◼ Gentle ascent (250 feet elevation gain)
High point ◼ 4700 feet
Hikable ◼ July through October
Contact ◼ Middle Fork Ranger District, (541) 782-2283

Three mountain lakes are perfectly spaced along a moderately graded trail, as if custom-ordered by a hiking family. The first lake is a pleasant 1.75 miles in, then 0.5 mile to the next, and 0.5 mile to the one after that. Middle Erma Bell is a beauty, and it's the best place to pause and picnic with children; the shoreline is gentle, neither rocky like the lower sister nor mucky like the upper. It's a popular trail; consider hiking it in autumn, when the huckleberry and vine maple are ablaze

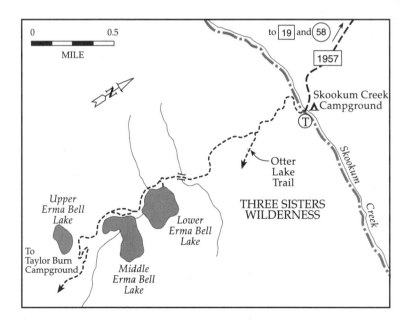

Lower Erma Bell Lake

with color and fellow hikers are few. Camping within 250 feet of any of the three lakes is restricted to a few spots marked with a post.

From Eugene follow State Highway 58 southeast for 40 miles and turn north at the sign to Westfir, just west of Oakridge. Drive 0.4 mile, turn left, and continue 32.4 miles up North Fork Road (Forest Road 19). At Box Canyon turn right on gravel Forest Road 1957 and drive 3.7 miles to Skookum Creek Campground and the trailhead.

Cross Skookum Creek on a wide footbridge and immediately enter Three Sisters Wilderness. At 0.5 mile bear right at the junction with Otter Lake Trail. Continue climbing gently; at about 1 mile descend for 0.3 mile or so, cross a creek, climb again, and at 1.75 mile reach a fork; Lower Erma Bell lies about 80 yards down the spur trail to the left. Watch for water ouzels flitting about the scree-covered southern shoreline.

Back on the main trail, cross the outlet for Lower Erma Bell Lake and follow the trail along the lake's edge, climbing gently through an impressive rhododendron grove. Lower Erma Bell is still in sight when Middle Erma Bell comes into view. A spur trail leads down to Middle Erma Bell; the main trail continues past the lake, granting only glimmering glimpses of it through the forest.

About a minute after the middle lake can no longer be seen, Upper Erma Bell comes into view—the smallest of the three lakes, not much more than a pond. The trail continues 1.75 miles to Taylor Burn Campground, a rough 8-mile drive north of Waldo Lake.

For more fun exploring: On the drive in or out, stop to explore the "old" cabin near the road in Box Canyon. It's really a replica of Landis Cabin, built here in 1918 as a Forest Service fire guard station. Vandals destroyed the original cabin in 1969; its replica was built in 1972.

45 LARISON COVE

Type	▪ Day hike or backpack
Difficulty	▪ Easy to moderate for children
Distance	▪ 4 miles round trip
Terrain	▪ Nearly level
High point	▪ 1600 feet
Hikable	▪ Year-round
FYI	▪ Trail shared with bikes
Contact	▪ Middle Fork Ranger District, (541) 782-2283

Just outside of Oakridge, Hills Creek Reservoir stretches to the south, reaching its many arms into mountain creek valleys and creating isolated coves. One particularly long cove, Larison, has an easy, quietly scenic trail following its north bank. No motorized boats are allowed

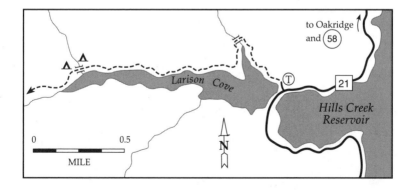

on this cove. In fact, picnic areas have been developed on the south shore specifically to encourage canoeing, adding to the peaceful charm of the trail. The entire trail is more than 6 miles long, but most families will stop at the footbridge at the 2-mile point, near the head of the cove. Picnic here, or overnight at one of the campsites on either side of the side creek. (There's a pit toilet near the footbridge, too.)

About 1 mile east of Oakridge (about 40 miles southeast of Eugene on State Highway 58), turn south at the sign to Kitson Springs Road. Drive 0.5 mile and turn right onto Forest Road 21, crossing the Middle Fork of the Willamette, then bearing left with the main road and continuing 3.4 miles to the Larison Cove trailhead parking area, on your right. Watch carefully for mountain bikes as you hike (though most people explore this trail on foot).

Just past the trailhead a couple of spurs lead to the water's edge; keep them in mind for cooling off on the return, though the muddy lake bottom and slight drop-off make these less-than-ideal swimming spots. Continuing up the trail, watch for poison oak. At about 0.5 mile the trail leads a short distance up a cool side-creek canyon to cross the creek on a railed log bridge. The trail then returns to the shoreline, usually staying about 50 feet above the water. Old-growth

Crossing side creek on Larison Cove Trail

forest offers shade much of the way, though open stretches can be hot in summer.

At 2 miles the trail passes a campsite shortly before reaching a second footbridge crossing another side creek. A second campsite is just across the creek. The head of the cove, where the reservoir ends and Larison Creek begins, is about 0.2 mile beyond the footbridge, for hikers interested in more exploring.

46 SALT CREEK FALLS–DIAMOND CREEK FALLS

Type ▪	Day hike
Difficulty ▪	Easy to moderate for children
Distance ▪	3.25 miles, loop
Terrain ▪	Rolling (450 feet elevation gain)
Hikable ▪	June through October
High point ▪	4000 feet
Contact ▪	Middle Fork Ranger District, (541) 782-2283

This loop hike begins and ends at one of the Northwest's most impressive waterfalls and includes yet another dramatic falls at the loop's far end. It's a fun trail with a lot of interesting stops along the way, including a visit to a lake named Too Much Bear (what's the story there?). With so many rhododendrons, June is a particularly nice month for this hike.

From Oakridge (about 40 miles southeast of Eugene on State Highway 58), continue southeast on State 58 about 24 miles. About 1 mile after passing through a tunnel, make a sharp right on Forest Road 5893, at the sign to Salt Creek Falls, and follow it a short distance to the picnic area.

Begin the outing with a walk down a short, paved path to view 286-foot Salt Creek Falls, which begins as a slide down a 50-foot cliff and ends with a dramatic free fall. Back at the picnic area, follow the paved path upstream a short distance to a footbridge crossing Salt Creek, then bear right. In about 50 yards signs indicate the start of the loop trail. Head counterclockwise (on Diamond Creek Falls Trail) to start the hike with a glimpse into Salt Creek Canyon from the other side of the creek.

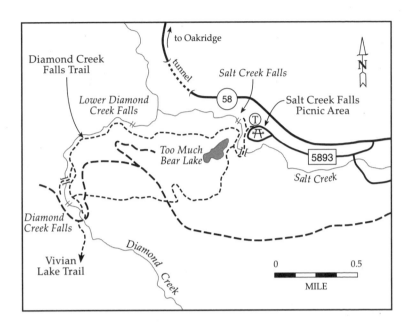

After a short climb, the trail reaches a viewpoint atop a cliff of basalt columns; the columns create a cobblestonelike surface, kind of interesting (and a little treacherous) for kids, given the sheer drop-off. Too Much Bear Lake lies just down the trail, off to the left; it's a small, oval, shallow stagnant pond ripe with potential for shoreline biological investigations.

A signed viewpoint at 0.3 mile leads to a view of the highway tunnel and sinuous creek canyon. The trail continues to roll through a forest of rhododendrons to a "viewpoint" at Lower Diamond Creek Falls at 0.7 mile. Trees obscure the view of this 200-foot falls, but this is the best view possible from the trail (though children will hear its roar as they approach and pass above it, at about 1 mile). Continue up gurgling Diamond Creek, passing a couple of clearcuts filled with rhododendrons. The trail steepens for about 0.2 mile just before, at 1.4 miles from the trailhead, it reaches the spur trail to Diamond Creek Falls. Follow this a short distance into the canyon, down a notched-log staircase, over a wide log bridge across the creek, and around the corner to see the 80-foot falls.

Back on the main trail, continue 0.2 mile to the junction with Vivian Lake Trail and bear left. Immediately cross a gravel road. From the junction, the trail mostly climbs gently for about 0.5 mile, then

Footbridge along Salt Creek Falls–Diamond Creek Falls loop

starts dropping through the forest of Douglas fir, hemlock, and rhododendrons, crossing the road once again. It ends back at the lower junction with Diamond Creek Falls Trail, about 1.2 miles from the upper trail junction. Continue back across Salt Creek to the picnic area.

47 MARILYN LAKES

Type ▪	Day hike or backpack
Difficulty ▪	Easy for children
Distance ▪	0.5 to 2 miles round trip
Terrain ▪	Gentle ascent (200 feet elevation gain)
High point ▪	5000 feet
Hikable ▪	July through October
Contact ▪	Middle Fork Ranger District, (541) 782-2283

Two sister lakes make a fine destination for a short hike with young children. Walk out and back from Gold Lake (a pleasant spot for a summer camping weekend) or from the lower trailhead (just 0.25 mile from the first lake), do a loop hike (returning on the road), or shuttle the kids back with a one-way hike on the 1.25-mile trail. A campsite at Upper Marilyn Lake makes an overnight trip possible; your child's first?

From Oakridge (about 40 miles southeast of Eugene on State Highway 58), continue southeast on State 58 some 25 miles to gravel Gold Lake Road (Forest Road 500). Follow it 1.2 miles to the lower trailhead, on the left. The upper trailhead is 0.8 mile farther, at Gold Lake Campground.

From the lower trailhead, Upper Marilyn Lake is just 0.25 mile down the trail through lush forest. The shore isn't particularly accessible at this end, although it's sunny and grassy and looks inviting for picnics. The trail gets very close to the shore as it continues around the lake's east side.

At 0.5 mile cross a short puncheon bridge over a bog. The trail veers away from the lake, then into the woods, and hits a junction at 0.75 mile. Go left to Lower Marilyn Lake, about 150 yards away, or right to Gold Lake, 0.5 mile farther through airy woods.

There's a campsite at Upper Marilyn Lake and what looks like the beginning of a trail around the lake, but it fades quickly. Bushwhackers in the group might have fun pushing farther around the lake.

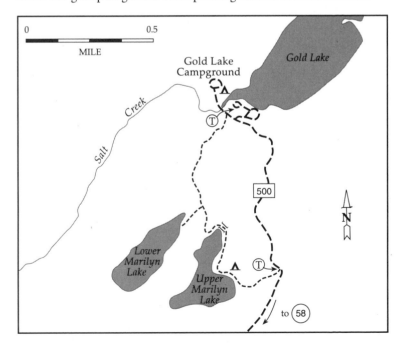

Upper Marilyn Lake

48 BOBBY LAKE

Type ▪	Day hike or backpack
Difficulty ▪	Moderate for children
Distance ▪	4.6 miles round trip
Terrain ▪	Nearly level (100 feet elevation gain)
Hikable ▪	July through October
High point ▪	5600 feet
Contact ▪	Middle Fork Ranger District, (541) 782-2283

Bobby Lake is one of dozens of lakes dotting the forest around Waldo Lake. The hike in is nearly level, though rather uneventful, and the good-size lake offers fine swimming and even decent fishing. Try to get in by late morning to soak up some sun on the big rock slab tilting into the lake's west end. The final 0.25 mile to Bobby Lake

Bobby Lake

follows a chunk of the Pacific Crest Trail (PCT); you may even meet up with some long-distance trekkers who might share some of their experiences with you.

   From Oakridge (about 40 miles southeast of Eugene on State Highway 58), continue on State 58 southeast 22 miles and turn north onto Waldo Lake Road (Forest Road 5897). Follow it 5.5 miles to a wide signed turnout on the left.

The route to Bobby Lake begins across the road on a wide trail through airy woods; it's flat or gently rolling the entire route. At 0.4 mile you will arrive at a junction with Gold Lake Trail; go straight. The trail continues its fairly straight route, without many distractions, to its junction with the PCT at 2 miles. Turn left; the lake is ahead 0.8 mile. Bear right at a fork to get right to the lake; continue

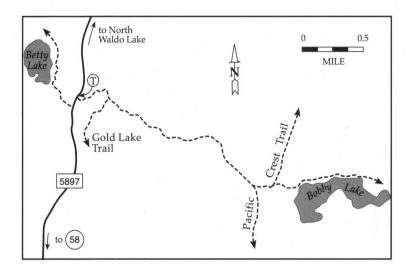

around to the right to get to the big rock. The trail continues along the lake's north shore and on into Deschutes National Forest. Return as you came.

For more fun exploring: Back at the trailhead, any hikers needing to work off more energy can continue across the road and stroll over to pretty Betty Lake, 0.4 mile west of the road.

49 SOUTH WALDO SHELTER

Type ▪	Day hike or backpack
Difficulty ▪	Easy to moderate for children
Distance ▪	3.4 miles round trip
Terrain ▪	Nearly level
High point ▪	5400 feet
Hikable ▪	July through October
Contact ▪	Middle Fork Ranger District, (541) 782-2283

At 10 square miles, Waldo Lake is the second-largest lake in Oregon and is considered by scientists to be perhaps the purest large lake in the world. It's a grand place in late summer, when the swarms of mosquitoes that plague campers in early summer are gone. A 21.8-mile trail encircles the entire lake; this short, level stretch offers excellent views of the lake and nice camping.

From Oakridge (about 40 miles southeast of Eugene on State Highway 58), continue on State 58 southeast 22 miles to Waldo Lake Road (Forest Road 5897). Drive 7 miles, turn left on Forest Road 5896 at the sign to Shadow Bay Campground, and follow signs to the boat ramp.

A trail sign points toward the bay, where a crescent of smooth, white sand beckons. If hikers can tear themselves away, pick up the trail heading south, following it around Shadow Bay and crossing a couple of small bridges in the process. At 0.4 mile the trail joins the main Waldo Lake Trail and, shortly thereafter, enters Waldo Lake Wilderness.

About this point, pause to see if anything seems different. It should: The trail is now beyond the protection of the bay, and even on a gentle day hikers should be feeling the wind across the lake and seeing waves lapping at the shore. Soon the trail crosses a substantial footbridge, then leads through a bog filled with skunk cabbage and, at 1 mile, crosses another beefy bridge, and then another.

Here look for a particularly pretty beach; on hot summer days, its gentle surf is reminiscent of a tropical beach. Eventually the terrain

South Waldo Shelter

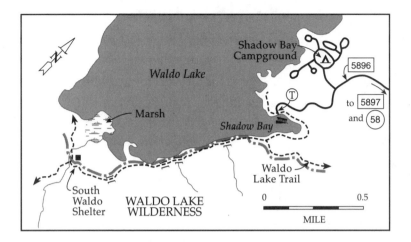

becomes more rolling, and at about 1.3 miles the trail swings out of sight of the lake to skirt a marsh. Cross one more big footbridge before reaching three-sided, shingle-roofed South Waldo Shelter at 1.7 miles.

The meadows here are inviting for camping, and the shelter itself might be a godsend on a rainy day. There are no bunks or stove, but there's a fireplace in front. Turn around here or continue farther up the trail. Waldo Lake comes back into view in about 0.3 mile.

50 ISLET BEACH

Type ■	Day hike or backpack
Difficulty ■	Easy for children
Distance ■	2.5 miles round trip
Terrain ■	Nearly level
High point ■	5400 feet
Hikable ■	July through October
Contact ■	Middle Fork Ranger District, (541) 782-2283

Waldo Lake offers several swimming beaches accessible by road; Islet Beach requires a hike—a short one that's worth every step. A long, wide crescent of soft sand faces west and, on sunny days, is bathed in

Islet Beach

sun all afternoon long. The hike is an easy stroll through the woods, past several smaller beaches and coves—warm-up acts to the main event.

From Oakridge (about 40 miles southeast of Eugene on State Highway 58), continue on State 58 southeast 22 miles to the start of Waldo Lake Road (Forest Road 5897); drive 13 miles (becomes Forest Road 5898) and turn left at the sign to Islet Campground. Follow signs 1.2 miles to the boat ramp and look for the trail sign.

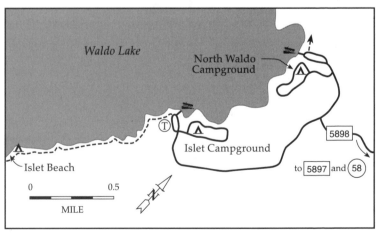

Hike south on the shoreline trail. (The main Waldo Lake Trail circling the lake is far from the lake at this point.) Immediately the trail passes a small gray-sand beach, then a small cove at 0.2 mile, then another small beach at 0.9 mile—all worth a stop. The trail ends at Islet Beach, some 75 sandy yards long. Look for a campsite on a promontory overlooking the lake just north of the beach.

51 RIGDON LAKES

Type ▪	Day hike
Difficulty ▪	Moderate for children
Distance ▪	4.8 miles round trip
Terrain ▪	Nearly level (200 feet elevation gain)
High point ▪	5500 feet
Hikable ▪	July through October
Contact ▪	Middle Fork Ranger District, (541) 782-2283

The hike into Rigdon Lakes is nearly flat; a couple of trail-side ponds help tick off the miles and provide an excuse to pause and explore.

From Oakridge (about 40 miles southeast of Eugene on State Highway 58), continue on State 58 southeast 22 miles to the start of

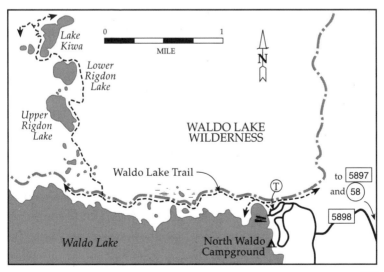

Upper Rigdon Lake

Waldo Lake Road (Forest Road 5897); drive 13 miles (becomes Forest Road 5898) and turn right at the sign to North Waldo Campground. Continue 0.8 mile, following signs to the boating and swimming area at North Waldo. The trail begins off the lower end of the parking area, near the rest rooms.

From the trailhead, walk 0.1 mile before the main Waldo Lake Trail comes in from the right, then bear right as the shoreline trail veers off to the left. Alternately, take the shoreline trail for better views; it rejoins the main trail in one mile, adding 0.6 mile to the round trip hike. The trail rolls through the mountain hemlock forest, which effectively blocks any view of Waldo Lake. At 1 mile, notice the small pond—or, later in the season, marsh—on your right; it marks the halfway point to the first Rigdon Lake. Soon the trail passes another big pond on the left and a smaller one on the right. At 1.7 miles the trail for Rigdon Lakes takes off to the right (the main trail continues around the lake).

From the junction, walk 0.3 mile to an unsigned fork and bear left to reach Upper Rigdon Lake in a few steps. Approach quietly; you may see birds resting on the lake. Although the lake is pretty, the shoreline isn't terribly inviting. Return to the main trail and continue another 0.4 mile to Lower Rigdon Lake. Its shoreline isn't much flatter, but it is shallow around the edge, inviting kids with old sneakers or aqua socks to wade in and try to catch water skeeter bugs and other shoreline critters.

If a 4.8-mile round trip isn't enough for your party, it's not far to a
third lake, Kiwa. Camping isn't permitted within 100 feet of any of
the three lakes; consider camping at North Waldo Campground and
day hiking into these lakes.

52 ROSARY LAKES

Type ■	Day hike or backpack
Difficulty ■	Strenuous for children
Distance ■	7 miles round trip
Terrain ■	Gradual ascent (800 feet elevation gain)
High point ■	5880 feet
Hikable ■	July through October
Contact ■	Middle Fork Ranger District, (541) 782-2283

The Rosary Lakes, just east of the crest of the Cascades, are what
they sound like: a succession of three emerald lakes strung close together in deep forest. The most difficult part of the hike is the initial
2.7 miles to the first lake; it's not steep, just not terribly interesting.
Keep eyes peeled for glimpses of Odell Lake through the trees to the
south. If kids are old enough to handle a hike this long, they'll be
glad they did: the closely set lakes are fun for brisk dips and even
trout fishing. Carry river shoes to wear into the muddy lakes.

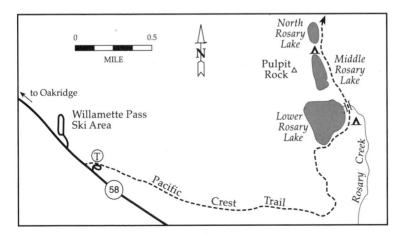

Middle Rosary Lake

Just past Willamette Pass Ski Area on State Highway 58 (about 29 miles southeast of Oakridge), turn left at the small hiker sign. Bear right at the highway maintenance shed and gravel pit and park at the far end of the parking area, where the trail begins.

The route follows the Pacific Crest Trail through an airy pine-and-fir forest on a gentle but steady incline for 2.7 miles before sneaking up on Lower Rosary Lake, a medium-size mountain lake with a scree slope on its far side. The trail continues around the lake's gentle south shore, passing campsites on a flat above the lake. At 3 miles cross a bridge over the lower lake's outlet, then start uphill toward Middle Rosary Lake, about 0.4 mile farther. North Rosary Lake is at 3.5 miles, just across a narrow band of forest from its sister. Return as you came.

Union Creek Trail

SOUTHERN CASCADES AND SISKIYOUS

53 FERN FALLS

Type ■ Day hike
Difficulty ■ Easy for children
Distance ■ 3.5 miles round trip
Terrain ■ Nearly level
High point ■ 840 feet
Hikable ■ Year-round
Contact ■ Bureau of Land Management, Roseburg office, (541) 672-4491

The 76-mile North Umpqua Trail is one of several long-distance riverside trails in western Oregon. The lower end of the trail—which begins at Swiftwater Bridge, 21 miles east of Roseburg—is particularly appealing to families, as it provides year-round hiking opportunities on gentle grades. Here the trail follows the river's south bank, opposite State Highway 138; road bridges at four points divide the trail into three sections ranging from 5 miles to 15.7 miles in length.

The lowest section is a long one, too long for a day hike with kids. However, it lends itself to an out-and-back hike to Fern Falls that's accessible all year. Try other trail sections as time and curiosity lead you. Each section has its own rewards; maps detailing the entire trail as well as trail guides describing each section are available from local Forest Service and Bureau of Land Management offices.

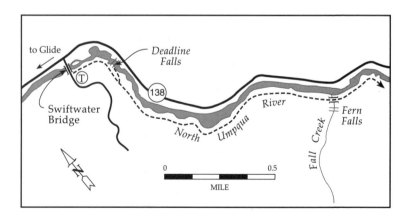

Fern Falls

From Glide (15 miles east of Roseburg), drive east 6 miles on State Highway 138 to Swiftwater Bridge, west of milepost 22. The trail starts just across the bridge on the upstream side. The next access point is in 15.7 miles, at Wright Creek Bridge.

From Swiftwater Bridge hike up the nearly level trail 0.25 mile to a spur on the left, leading to a view of Deadline Falls. Here, especially from May through September, watch for anadromous (migrating) fish—Chinook and coho salmon, plus steelhead trout—attempting to jump the falls. The trail continues into a gorgeous forest dripping with moss, crossing little side creeks. You will discover many places to scramble down to the rushing North Umpqua River. Stay on the lookout for poison oak all along the trail. At 1.75 miles the trail crosses Fall Creek on a laminated wood footbridge at Fern Falls. Under the bridge, the creek spreads out in a shallow, rocky fan, inviting for water play. Continue up the trail, or turn around and return the way you came.

54 SUSAN CREEK FALLS

Type ▪ Day hike
Difficulty ▪ Easy for children
Distance ▪ 1 mile round trip
Terrain ▪ Gradual ascent (120 feet elevation gain)
High point ▪ 1060 feet
Hikable ▪ Year-round
Contact ▪ Bureau of Land Management, Roseburg office, (541) 672-4491

The North Umpqua corridor offers a wealth of short waterfall hikes, ideal for families with young children. As an alternative to one long

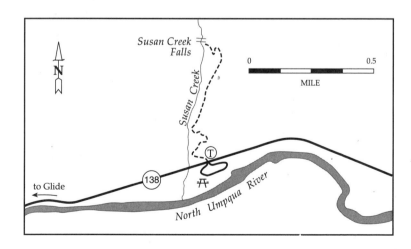

day hike, consider driving up State Highway 138, stopping to take in two or three short hikes. Put Susan Creek Falls at the top of your list. From Roseburg you can drive to the trailhead in about a half-hour, and its low elevation means spring and its wildflowers come early.

From Glide (15 miles east of Roseburg), take State 138 east 12 miles to the Susan Creek Falls trailhead. The trail starts on the north side of the highway, but parking is on the south, in a picnic area.

Follow the trail through deep forest east of the creek. The trail ends at the base of the falls, which tumbles 60 feet into a punch bowl. Encourage children to look for dippers, or water ouzels—small, dark-gray birds adapted to life in and around mountain streams. They often build nests right on the edge of waterfalls, and they're frequently seen at Susan Creek Falls dipping in the spray and walking under the stream. Return as you came.

Susan Creek

55 FALL CREEK FALLS

Type ▪	Day hike
Difficulty ▪	Easy for children
Distance ▪	1.8 miles round trip
Terrain ▪	Nearly level or steady ascent (380 feet elevation gain)
High point ▪	1400 feet
Hikable ▪	Year-round
Contact ▪	North Umpqua Ranger District, (541) 496-3532

It's easy to keep kids interested along this short trail, from the wooden bridge at the trailhead to the viewing platform part way up the falls. Spring brings an array of woodland wildflowers to the trail's borders, further enhancing a hike here.

From Glide (15 miles east of Roseburg), drive east 16.5 miles on State Highway 138 to the signed trailhead parking lot, on the left.

From the trailhead, immediately cross Fall Creek on a wooden bridge, then pass through a cut in a tree that appears to have fallen across the trail—an opportunity to talk about assessing a tree's age from the growth rings. (If children are overwhelmed by counting the rings, look for the rings which, had the tree fallen today, would indicate the years they were born.)

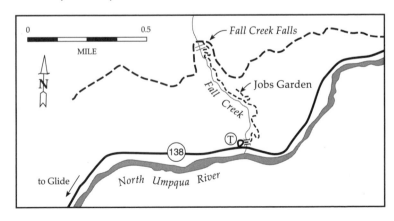

Fall Creek Falls

Just up the trail, squeeze through a crevice in a rock the size of a small house. The trail continues close to the creek, which spills and froths over mossy boulders. It switchbacks uphill briefly; then, at about 0.5 mile, a spur trail takes off to the right, leading in 0.1 mile to Jobs Garden (an area of unusual rock formations). There's plenty of poison oak here, so watch the children and stay on the trail. As the creek flattens, the trail levels out and veers away from it, still staying within earshot.

At about 0.8 mile the trail rejoins the creek, now flat and quiet, just before reaching the falls. Here the creek twists around a corner, then showers down a rock face, falling nearly 100 feet in the process. A slippery log crosses the creek just downstream of the falls—fun to walk on, but hazardous without close supervision. The trail continues up the hill next to the falls, switchbacking four more times to the top of the falls. It's a fun way to work off a little extra energy, but there's not much to see at the top, though there's a nice intermediate viewpoint along the way. The trail ends at a gravel road atop the falls. Return as you came.

56 TOKETEE AND WATSON FALLS

Type ▪ Day hike
Hikable ▪ Most of the year
Contact ▪ Diamond Lake Ranger District, (541) 498-2531

TOKETEE FALLS

Difficulty ▪ Easy for children
Distance ▪ 1 mile round trip
Terrain ▪ Level, plus short, steep ascent (100 feet elevation gain)
High point ▪ 2360 feet

WATSON FALLS

Difficulty ▪ Easy for children
Distance ▪ 1 mile round trip
Terrain ▪ Short, steep ascent (280 feet elevation gain)
High point ▪ 3040 feet

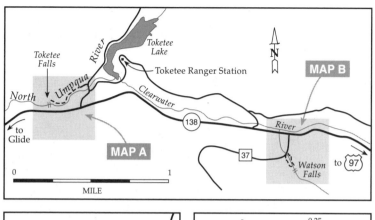

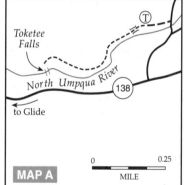

Trailheads for these two short hikes are just about 2 miles apart; pair them and you'll have 2 miles of hiking and some of southern Oregon's best waterfall views. Both are just off State Highway 138, about a 45-minute drive past Glide.

Toketee Falls is probably the most dramatic of the North Umpqua corridor falls, especially viewed as hikers do—across a chasm from a platform clinging to a cliff. Children will enjoy watching the water burble and swirl in the creek alongside the trail as it approaches the falls. The narrow tread and steep drop-offs urge caution with young children, however.

The trail at 272-foot Watson Falls follows the steep, crashing creek up to a series of wooden viewing platforms. You can see the top of the falls from the parking area, but it's nothing compared to the view you get by walking a few minutes. The climb is rather steep, but views of the falls tease even reluctant hikers to the top.

Watson Falls

TOKATEE FALLS

From Glide drive east on State Highway 138 about 40 miles and turn north at the west entrance to Toketee Ranger Station (milepost 59). Turn left, cross a bridge, turn left again, and then drive a short distance to the trailhead. (That huge, dripping redwood pipe you see next to the trailhead is used to divert water from nearby Toketee Lake and carry it to another pipe, where it drops steeply to a powerhouse to make electricity.)

Cross a footbridge and walk the level path through the forest, passing several potential picnic sites along the river. The trail then starts to climb a bit on sturdy stone steps. Peek down to the left at the gorgeous deep pools in the creek along the trail. Hikers may want to wander off the trail to play in a safe spot along the creek. Approaching the end, the trail drops about 100 feet to a viewing platform perched on the side of the canyon. Look across a wide gulf to see the North Umpqua River pouring through a cleft in a wall of columnar basalt and dropping some 90 feet into an emerald pool. Return as you came.

WATSON FALLS

Continue on State 138 and turn right on Forest Road 37 (between mileposts 61 and 62). Drive 0.1 mile to the large, signed parking area on the right. Signs lead hikers up across Road 37 and onto a footpath ascending the hillside across the road. The route is rather steep, sticking close to the creek as it runs noisily over mossy boulders down out of the mountains. The first trail-side view of the falls comes at about 0.25 mile. Keep going to a railed wooden platform zigzagging over the creek near the base of the falls. Continue up the trail on another switchback for a better view of the falls, then up yet another switchback to reach the highest viewpoint, poised about one-third of the way up the falls in a magnificent natural amphitheater of gray and pale green rock and moss. The cataract falls straight down a cliff, pounding a pile of boulders and vaporizing into clouds of mist. To return, follow signs to the "return trail" spur that starts just east of the railed platform bridge. It takes a slightly steeper, quicker route back to the parking area.

57 CLEETWOOD COVE

Type	■ Day hike
Difficulty	■ Moderate for children
Distance	■ 2.2 miles round trip
Terrain	■ Steady ascent (760 feet elevation gain)
High point	■ 6935 feet
Hikable	■ July through October
FYI	■ No dogs allowed
Contact	■ Crater Lake National Park, (541) 594-2211, ext. 402

Thousands of people drive around the rim of Crater Lake, gazing across its deep, clear blue waters, but far fewer actually dip their toes in it. There's only one way to get to the lake, and that's with a hike down the Cleetwood Trail. Boat tours to Wizard Island leave from the dock at the trail's end; call park headquarters for the schedule. Even without the boat ride, the hike is worthwhile, especially if it's hot enough to justify a dive into the bone-chilling lake.

From the western border of Crater Lake National Park (70 miles northeast of Medford), continue east approximately 7 miles on State

Highway 62 and turn left toward park headquarters. In 4 miles turn left on Rim Drive and drive 3 miles to Rim Village. The trailhead is almost directly across the lake from Rim Village (clockwise 10.6 miles on the rim road). Park across the road from the trailhead in the large parking area.

The wide trail's descent isn't really steep, but it's steady. Benches are scattered all along the trail. (The prospect of a boat tour motivates a lot of less-than-fit tourists to walk this trail; they make good use of the opportunities to rest.) The lake glimmers along the trail all the way down the long switchbacks.

The trail ends at the little boat dock. Sit on the edge of the dock, dipping your feet, or pick your way along the boulder-strewn shore to find a picnic or wading spot. Bring old sneakers or aqua socks for wading, as the rocks can be sharp.

For more fun exploring: Thanks to well-informed guides, the boat tour is a great way to learn about the geologic forces that created

Cleetwood Cove dock on Crater Lake

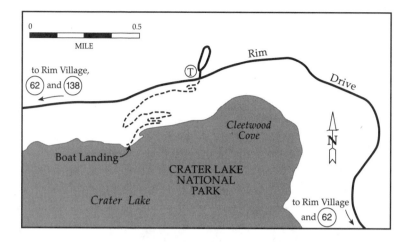

Crater Lake and the landmarks around the rim. At Wizard Island you can get out and hike 0.9 mile (and 764 feet) up to the top of the island, catching another boat to return—assuming there's room; it's a little chancy (see Hike 58 map).

58 THE WATCHMAN

Type ▪	Day hike
Difficulty ▪	Easy to moderate for children
Distance ▪	1.4 miles round trip
Terrain ▪	Steady ascent (419 feet elevation gain)
High point ▪	8056 feet
Hikable ▪	July through October
FYI ▪	No dogs allowed
Contact ▪	Crater Lake National Park, (541) 594-2211, ext. 402

Don't visit Crater Lake without hiking down to the lake's edge at Cleetwood Cove (Hike 57) or up to a high point overlooking the lake. Several peaks with summit trails dot the rim. The Watchman is the shortest and easiest of the bunch, and still grants a dynamite bird's-eye view of the deep blue lake and the best view of Wizard Island, directly below.

Lookout atop The Watchman

 From Rim Village follow Rim Drive to the west and north 3.8 miles to the signed viewpoint and parking area at The Watchman. The trail starts just south of the parking area along the rim.

The trail begins with a long straightaway that gradually curves behind The Watchman peak. At about 0.5 mile the trail reaches a switchback—the first of a half-dozen switchbacks that come closer and closer together as you near the top. At the summit there's a fire lookout cabin, but no visitors are allowed inside. (With so many visitors, the person staffing the lookout would never get a chance to watch for fires.) Instead enjoy the view from the rock-walled viewpoint. Return as you came.

For more fun exploring: Older children seeking more challenge might enjoy Garfield Peak, a 3-mile round trip (980 feet elevation gain) that begins just behind Crater Lake Lodge, or Mount Scott, a 5-mile round trip (1326 feet elevation gain) directly across the lake from Rim Village.

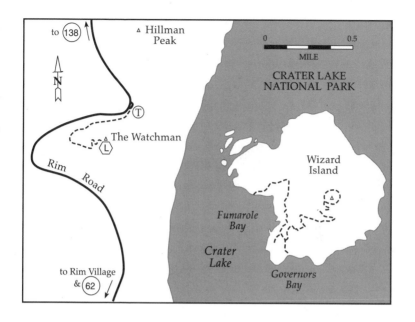

59 UNION CREEK

Type	■ Day hike
Difficulty	■ Easy to moderate for children
Distance	■ 4.4 miles one way
Terrain	■ Gentle ascent or descent (445 feet elevation gain)
High point	■ 3765 feet
Hikable	■ April through November
Contact	■ Prospect Ranger District, (541) 560-3623

Union Creek is the kind of trail that sneaks up on you. There are no dramatic vistas, just easy walking through a magnificent forest following a babbling creek. Start a one-way hike at the upper end with a splash (a view of pretty Union Falls) and end at the community of Union Creek. Or begin at Union Creek and wander upstream a mile or two, then turn around. In addition to huge, old-growth Douglas fir, there are hemlocks, sugar pines, alder, yew, and all kinds of wildflowers in late spring.

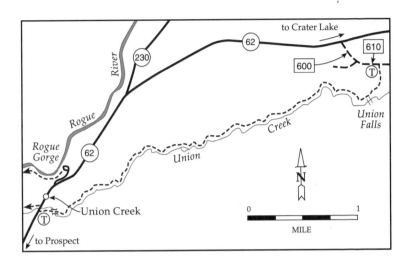

The lower trailhead is on the south side of the highway bridge over the creek at the community of Union Creek, which is 11 miles north of Prospect on State Highway 62. Follow the path up the east bank a short distance, cross the creek on a footbridge (slippery when wet), and continue up the west bank. To reach the upper trailhead, continue north from the community of Union Creek 3.3 miles on State 62 and turn right onto Forest Road 600 at the sign to the Union Creek trailhead. Go 0.2 mile and bear left onto Forest Road 610. The trailhead is on the right in 0.2 mile.

From the upper trailhead, walk through the level forest, listening for falls, then drop down the hillside to reach the base of Union Falls at 0.3 mile. Here the creek drops about 5 feet over a smooth lip, then churns and boils down several more ledges.

From the falls, the trail winds gently down along the north bank of Union Creek, usually in sight of the wide creek. Notice the moss-covered volcanic creek bed at the upper end; farther down, as the lava diminishes, the creek's edges are less well defined. Logs are strewn across the creek in many places, creating tempting footbridges and obscuring the creek in places. Point out to children the mid-stream islands; some appear to have started after a tree fell into the creek and other plants began to grow on the decaying tree. They also can see dry channels where apparently the creek was diverted by a logjam. What caused all those logs to fall into the creek? Logging operations, beavers, wind, and even the creek itself, undercutting the root systems of trees along its bank.

Union Creek Trail

After crossing the footbridge back at Union Creek, the trail reaches the highway at 4.4 miles, but it continues across the road another 0.4 mile to intersect the Rogue Gorge Trail. You'll want to visit Rogue Gorge while you're in the area; a short asphalt path leads past dramatic views of the Rogue River churning its way through a narrow lava chasm. Fencing and viewing platforms make it safe for even young children.

6O NATURAL BRIDGE

Type	▪ Day hike
Difficulty	▪ Easy for children
Distance	▪ 2 miles, loop
Terrain	▪ Rolling (200 feet elevation gain)
High point	▪ 3200 feet
Hikable	▪ Mid-May through mid-October
Contact	▪ Prospect Ranger District, (541) 560-3623

In its dash from the slopes of Crater Lake's Mount Mazama to the Pacific Ocean, the Rogue River does a sudden disappearing act,

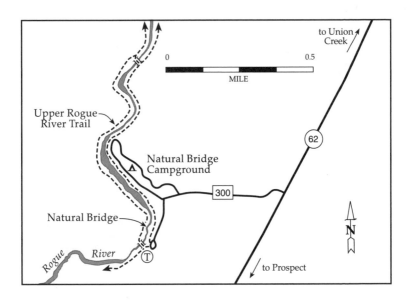

reappearing a short distance downstream. Where did it go? Into a series of lava tubes in the river's channel. The Forest Service has developed an excellent interpretive trail overlooking Natural Bridge that enlightens visitors and steers them safely away from walking on Natural Bridge itself. Link that short, paved path with forest trails on either side of the river, throw in a pair of footbridges, and what results is a wonderful, generally uncrowded loop hike. The east-bank trail section skirts a busy campground, but the west-bank section is little used.

The trail is generally snow-free from April through November, but the road to Natural Bridge is open only mid-May through mid-October. It's possible to catch the loop by walking the 0.5 mile in from the highway or, better yet, hiking down 1.5 miles from Union Creek on the east-bank trail. You may even have the entire trail to yourself.

From Union Creek (11 miles north of Prospect), drive south 1 mile on State Highway 62 and turn west at the sign to Natural Bridge onto Forest Road 300. Continue 0.5 mile, bearing left at the Y, and park at the day-use area.

Walk past the kiosk with interpretive signs to get on a paved path leading to a dramatic metal footbridge spanning the churning Rogue River. The path then winds upstream, safely fenced off from steep cliffs, with several overlooks and signs explaining the geologic processes that created the scene below. The paved path ends at a view of

Natural Bridge, but the trail—Upper Rogue River Trail—continues as a dirt footpath. It follows a level course for about 0.25 mile, then climbs perhaps 200 feet above the river in deep woods. Look down and see the now peacefully flowing green river between the trees.

After a while you will glimpse tents and trailers parked in the campground across the river, then a bright, bleached, wooden footbridge below. The trail seems to overshoot the footbridge as it drops to river level, but a right turn at a trail junction leads along a quaint, rock-lined path back to the bridge. Cross it and turn right. (A left turn leads 1.5 miles to Union Creek.) The north end of the campground is about 0.25 mile from the bridge. The trail here threads between river and campground for 0.5 mile or so; notice the river's initial calm, then its growing sense of urgency, as it narrows and drops toward Natural Bridge. For the last 0.25 mile the trail veers away from the river and into the woods, ending at the viewpoint parking area.

Footbridge at Natural Bridge, Rogue River

61 TAKELMA GORGE

Type ■ Day hike
Difficulty ■ Moderate for children
Distance ■ 2.8 to 3.8 miles round trip
Terrain ■ Nearly level (120 feet elevation gain)
High point ■ 2960 feet
Hikable ■ Most of the year
Contact ■ Prospect Ranger District, (541) 560-3623

The 48-mile-long Upper Rogue River Trail follows the river from the town of Prospect upstream to Crater Rim Viewpoint, just outside

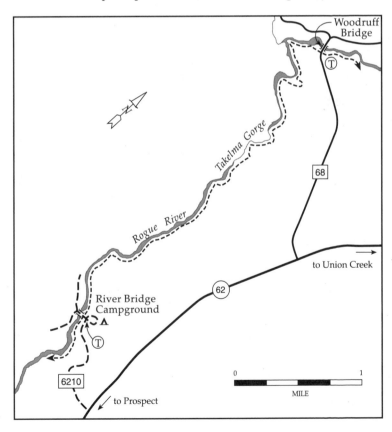

Takelma Gorge

Crater Lake National Park, providing a lot of options for relatively easy one-way and round-trip hikes. Two of those options appear in this book: Hike 60 (Natural Bridge Loop) and this one, a hike to dramatic Takelma Gorge. Hike out to the gorge and back from Woodruff Bridge; alternately, leave a shuttle car at River Bridge Campround and hike 4.6 miles one way from Woodruff Bridge.

From Union Creek, drive 4.7 miles south on State Highway 62 and turn right at the sign to Woodruff Bridge onto Forest Road 68. Continue 2 miles and park on the left just before the bridge.

Head south on Upper Rogue River Trail; the river reappears in 0.25 mile, flowing placidly here. The trail continues downstream, mostly level with a few ups and downs, with the river mostly out of sight. At about 1 mile the river can be heard and seen quickening its pace, as if it were anticipating the gorge ahead. The trail grows rockier where it passes atop basalt-column cliffs; look across the river to see similar cliffs. Is this the gorge? Not quite; it's obvious when it appears. Continue another 0.4 mile and there it is: a channel of white water turning sharply and roaring between vertical cliffs of dark basalt, under logs swept downstream and lodged between the gorge walls.

Turn around here or continue along the top of the 0.5-mile gorge before returning. Below the gorge the river flattens again, and it's a mellow 2.5 miles to River Bridge Campground. To leave a car at this end, take State 62 south 2.2 miles from the Woodruff Bridge turnoff, turn right on gravel Road 6210, and follow it 1 mile to the campground.

62 UPPER TABLE ROCK

Type ■ Day hike
Difficulty ■ Moderate for children
Distance ■ 2.5 miles round trip
Terrain ■ Steady, sometimes steep ascent (800 feet elevation gain)
High point ■ 2050 feet
Hikable ■ Year-round
FYI ■ No camping, no dogs allowed
Contact ■ Bureau of Land Management, Medford, (541) 770-2200

Anyone who has driven past Medford on I-5 has noticed the pair of flattop mesas north of the freeway. Both Upper and Lower Table Rock have trails to their summits; the trail that ascends Upper Table Rock is shorter, a little less steep, and a bit more open for views. It's a good wildflower walk in spring, but children will be more intrigued by the summit, which is literally flat enough to land a plane on. The grassy summit is a bit boggy in winter and spring; in summer, go

Upper Table Rock

early in the day, before the heat becomes oppressive. In all seasons, beware of poison oak and (according to reports) rattlesnakes.

From I-5 in Medford take exit 33 (Central Point) and follow Biddle Road 0.8 mile to Table Rock Road. Turn left and drive 5.3 miles. Where the road swings to the left, turn right on Modoc Road and continue 1.5 miles to the signed trailhead, on the left.

Start up through a tangle of oak and madrona trees. The trail can be rocky in some places, muddy in others. It passes between huge

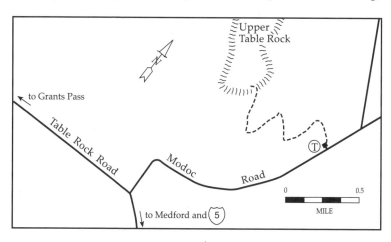

basalt outcrops at 0.2 mile. At 0.5 mile there's a bench inviting hikers to pause and enjoy the view of the Rogue River Valley. There's another bench at 0.9 mile, where the trail enters the forest and obscures the view the rest of the way to the summit. The upper part of the trail has some steep pitches. Quite suddenly, at 1.25 miles, the trail emerges onto the flat, open expanse at the top of the rock.

Even kids who have a hard time dragging themselves to the summit tend to become converts once they reach the summit, with its unusual open, flat, virtually treeless landscape. The trail hits the summit near one end of the horseshoe-shaped rock; head left to get to the end, or wander to the center of the horseshoe for a dramatic view of the rocky gorge below.

63 OREGON CAVES–BIG TREE LOOP

Type ■	Day hike
Difficulty ■	Moderate for children
Distance ■	3.3 miles, loop
Terrain ■	Steady, sometimes steep ascent (1100 feet elevation gain)
High point ■	5080 feet
Hikable ■	July through October
Contact ■	Oregon Caves National Monument, (541) 592-3400

Hikers in southern Oregon don't tend to think of the trails around Oregon Caves National Monument when choosing a destination, and tourists visiting the caves don't tend to be interested in hiking. The combination makes this interesting and moderately challenging loop trail uncrowded as well, despite its proximity to a popular tourist attraction. This hike, along with a tour of the caves, makes a full day's outing for a family. The complete loop is 3.3 miles, but an out-and-back hike to the huge Douglas fir is only 2.6 miles. Ask at the monument's information office about even shorter loop hikes in the caves area.

 From Cave Junction (southwest of Grants Pass on US Highway 199), follow State Highway 46 east 19 miles to the parking lot at

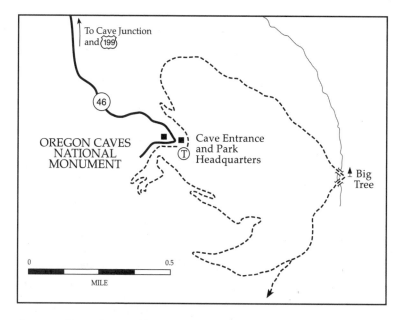

Oregon Caves National Monument. Walk up the road toward the cave entrance, then continue up the double staircases, past the ticket booth, and onto an asphalt path. Immediately the trail splits, signaling the start of the loop trail. Turn left for a more gradual approach to the Big Tree.

The trail quickly turns to dirt. The route, fairly steep for the first 0.4 mile, flattens out for a bit where the first of several trail-side benches appears. Then the trail makes a turn to the right; notice how the trees are bigger here and the forest cooler. At about 0.7 mile the trail gets steeper again and heads up steadily. In early July some pink rhododendrons may be in bloom. At 1.3 miles cross a tiny creek and immediately reach the Big Tree—a twelve-and-a-half-foot-thick Douglas fir, estimated to be 1200 to 1500 years old.

From here the trail continues up steadily another 0.4 mile to a junction; bear right and begin the descent. The trail cuts through a moist hillside where a profusion of flowers crowding the trail blooms in early summer; if the day is wet, hikers' legs will be, too. Swing down through the old-growth forest on long switchbacks. Suddenly, at about 3 miles, the trail emerges from the forest to offer a view over the shake-roofed Oregon Caves buildings, silvery in sunlight. The trail passes a couple of interpretive signs before turning to asphalt for the last 0.2 mile to the caves entrance area.

6₄ RAINIE FALLS

Type ▪	Day hike or backpack
Difficulty ▪	Easy to moderate for children
Distance ▪	3.6 miles round trip
Terrain ▪	Rolling after short, steep ascent (700 feet elevation gain)
High point ▪	790 feet
Hikable ▪	Year-round
Contact ▪	Smullen Visitor Center, (541) 479-3735

A wilderness river alternating between placid pools and wild white water, old cabins and archeological sites, and a benign climate are just a few of the attractions of the 40-mile Rogue River Trail. It's not as level as some riverside trails, but neither is it difficult, and attractions all along the way keep children interested—as long as the hike isn't attempted at midday in midsummer. Late spring is the ideal season to hike the Rogue River Trail. You may experience some showers or even a real storm, but weather tends to be pleasantly sunny and warm. Rainie Falls makes a good destination for a short hike with

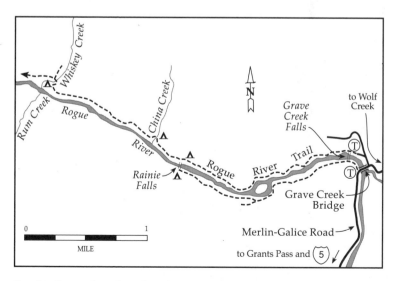

Entering Oregon Caves in early spring

children out of Grants Pass. Trails lead down both sides of the river from Grave Creek, where rafters put in for multiday trips into the wild canyon.

From I-5 just north of Grants Pass, take exit 61 (Merlin) and follow Merlin-Galice Road west 25 miles, past the town of Galice, to Grave Creek Bridge over the Rogue. Cross the bridge and take the spur road to the boat landing and trailhead on the left. (If you're planning an overnight trek, make arrangements with the Galice Resort to have your car shuttled back to Galice; it's illegal, and unwise, to leave a car at the landing overnight.)

From the boat landing, the Rogue River Trail starts up steeply, along a sheer slope overlooking the river, then levels out. At 0.6 mile look around to see the remains of an old miner's cabin. You will see another cabin across the river at 1.3 miles. Notice the concrete pier here; it was part of a stock bridge built in 1907 but destroyed in the flood of 1927. At 1.8 miles the trail reaches Rainie Falls, a dramatic 15- to 20-foot drop in the river. Hang around and you may see a party of boaters use ropes to line their rafts or drift boats down the narrow, more gradual channel along the north bank. A spur trail to the camping area is 0.1 mile back upstream.

Trail post along Rogue River Trail

Alternately, leave your car at the pullout at the east end of Grave Creek Bridge and walk the 2-mile south bank trail to the trail's end at Rainie Falls—a slightly rockier, rougher trail with some switchbacks, but one ending with an even better view of the falls.

For more fun exploring: If you hike the main north-side trail, don't stop at Rainie Falls; walk another 1.5 miles to

Whiskey Creek. The broad meadow and beach make it an appealing spot for a picnic and a popular spot for camping. There's another camping area 0.4 mile downstream, the last one for 2 miles. Check at Smullen Visitor Center, along the river between Galice and Grave Creek, for information about long-distance hikes or float trips down the Rogue.

65 GRIZZLY PEAK

Type ■ Day hike
Difficulty ■ Moderate for children
Distance ■ 3 miles round trip
Terrain ■ Rolling (660 feet elevation gain)
High point ■ 5922 feet
Hikable ■ April through October
Contact ■ Bureau of Land Management, Medford, (541) 770-2200

From downtown Ashland, look across the valley to the northeast: the tallest rise you see is Grizzly Peak. Imagine the view you'd get of Ashland from up there...or, better yet, hike up Grizzly Peak and see for yourself. The trail follows a gentle grade to an overlook below the summit; at this writing the Bureau of Land Management is working to add a loop trail from the main trail up to the summit (about 0.25 mile) and back.

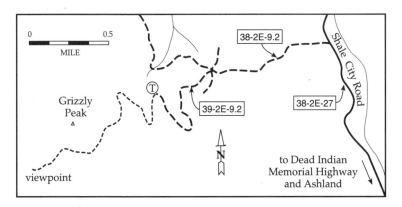

Viewpoint on Grizzly Peak

From I-5 at the south end of Ashland, take exit 14 and head east on State Highway 66 for 0.5 mile, then turn left on Dead Indian Memorial Highway. Follow the highway 6.7 miles and turn left on Shale City Road (BLM Road 38-2E-27), following signs to Grizzly Peak Trail. In about 3 miles turn left on BLM Road 38-2E-9.2. In 0.8 mile you'll reach a five-way intersection with power lines overhead; take the upper of two left forks onto Road 39-2E-9.2 (still following signs to the trail) and continue 1 mile to the trailhead at road's end. The trail immediately heads up, then moderates to switchback gently through deep forest. The last 0.5 mile of the 1.5-mile trail to the viewpoint overlooking Ashland is nearly level. Approaching the trail's end, you'll see spur trails on the right, leading toward the summit; the loop route here may be completed by the time you read this. Even if it's not completed, the grassy slopes leading to the summit are easy to explore off-trail. Otherwise, just perch on a rock at trail's end and drink in the view while you eat lunch, then return as you came.

Monkey Face, Smith Rock State Park

EAST OF THE
CASCADES

66 BLACK BUTTE

Type ▪ Day hike
Difficulty ▪ Moderate to strenuous for children
Distance ▪ 4 miles round trip
Terrain ▪ Steady ascent/descent (1640 feet elevation gain)
High point ▪ 6440 feet
Hikable ▪ June through October
Contact ▪ Sisters Ranger District, (541) 549-2111

Gaze at it from Black Butte Ranch resort, or drive by it on the highway, and the tall, black, symmetrical cinder cone of Black Butte just looks like something you'd want to climb. The road goes most of the way up; 2 miles of hiking finishes the ascent. On top is a veritable living museum of lookout towers, adding to the uniqueness of this hike.

 From the junction of State Highway 22 and US Highway 20/State Highway 126, drive east 20 miles and turn north on Indian Ford Road. In 0.2 mile bear left onto Green Ridge Road (Forest Road 11), drive 3.7 miles, and turn left on gravel Forest Road 1110. The ample trailhead parking area is ahead in 5.3 miles.

The route starts northward around the butte, ascending steadily through a forest of ponderosa pines. Small signs identify manzanita,

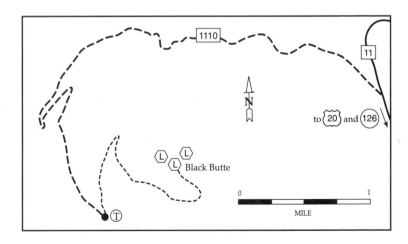

1924 lookout atop Black Butte

chinkapin, snowbrush, and other understory plants at trail side. At 0.6 mile the forest's character changes suddenly and becomes cooler as you enter a grove dominated by grand fir. Round a switchback at 0.8 mile and soon the trail emerges from the trees, granting views of Mount Washington and the Three Sisters. Look for scarlet gilia, balsam root, and other wildflowers on the open slopes here in midsummer.

The view just gets better and better—of nearby mountains as well as of the manicured fairways of the resort below. Just before climbing onto the summit, the trail enters a grove of subalpine fir, then passes through an old burn, evidence of the 1981 Black Butte fire. Look east to see Smith Rock jutting from the high desert floor.

Once on top, walk another minute to reach the base of an 85-foot lookout tower, built in 1934. There's plenty to see without climbing the tower, though it's hard to convince children of that (even with a sign that forbids it). Try redirecting children across the summit toward the 18-foot cupola lookout tower, built in 1924. A sign describes the development of fire lookout facilities on Black Butte, starting with an open platform constructed between two fir trees in 1910 and ending with the 1979 log cabin tucked just over the ridge near the cupola (occupied in summer, but not open to the public).

For more fun exploring: Most summers you'll find outfitters in the area offering trail rides through the ponderosa pines; call the Sisters Area Visitors Center at (541) 549-0251.

67 METOLIUS RIVER

Type ▪ Day hike
Difficulty ▪ Easy to moderate for children
Distance ▪ 5.4 miles round trip
Terrain ▪ Nearly level (150 feet elevation gain)
High point ▪ 2900 feet
Hikable ▪ Most of the year
Contact ▪ Sisters Ranger District, (541) 549-2111

The trail along the scenic Metolius River starts at a quiet, primitive campground, follows river grade most of the way, and hits Wizard Falls Fish Hatchery at 2.7 miles. Wizard Falls itself no longer exists; it was on a side creek, but disappeared in 1947 when water was diverted to the hatchery that took its name. Falls or no falls, it's an easy, lovely walk along a sometimes gentle, sometimes wild river, with a stroll through the fish hatchery a bonus. With a shuttle you could hike it one way.

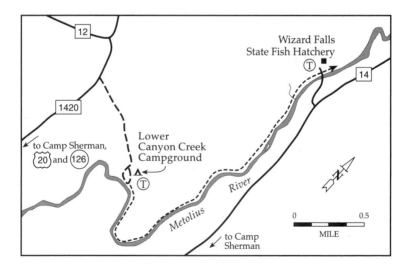

Display ponds at Wizard Falls Fish Hatchery

From US Highway 20, 9 miles west of Sisters, turn north at a sign for the Metolius River (Forest Road 1419). Follow Road 1419 (bearing left where a sign points right to campgrounds) to the stop sign at 4.8 miles. (If you reach the community of Camp Sherman, you've gone 0.5 mile too far.) At the stop sign go straight onto Forest Road 1420 and follow it 3.3 miles; turn right at the sign to Lower Canyon Creek Campground and continue 1 mile to the riverside trailhead in the small campground. (Alternately, begin at Wizard Falls Fish Hatchery, about 5 miles north of Camp Sherman off Forest Road 14.)

The trail begins at the far end of the campground, not more than a shrub's width from the river much of the way. Nowhere is the river shallow, narrow, or warm enough to cross, but safe (supervised) wading is possible in places. About 0.3 mile from the trailhead you'll spot springs bursting from the opposite riverbank and streaming into the river. In another 0.2 mile a long stretch of rapids begins. At about the halfway point the trail leaves the river's edge and gains a little elevation. At about 2 miles the river splits among brushy islands; you may see water ouzels here, as well as wildflowers early in summer. The hikers' trail returns to river level just 0.1 mile before reaching the fish hatchery (an alternative anglers' trail follows for some distance along the river below).

Take time to explore the hatchery, where six species of fish are reared. Display ponds grant close views of four of the six species found in the Metolius—rainbow trout, brown trout, kokanee, and brook trout. Bring quarters for the coin-operated fish food dispensers.

For more fun exploring: From Camp Sherman follow Forest Road 14 south about 2 miles to the head of the Metolius. A short walk rewards you with views of the river bursting forth from the hillside in a cold (48 degrees Fahrenheit) gush of water.

68 SMITH ROCK

Type ■ Day hike
Hikable ■ Most of the year
Contact ■ Smith Rock State Park, (541) 548-7501

RIVER PATH
Difficulty ■ Easy for children
Distance ■ 2.2 miles round trip
Terrain ■ Nearly level with short, steep ascent to parking (180 feet elevation gain)
High point ■ 2840 feet

MISERY RIDGE
Difficulty ■ Strenuous for children
Distance ■ 1.5 miles round trip
Terrain ■ Steep ascent (840 feet elevation gain)
High point ■ 3320 feet

Smith Rock draws climbers from around the world to tackle its steep, intricate pitches. Most of the cars in the parking lot seem to belong to climbers—and a few spectators who come to watch climbers spider their way up seemingly impossible routes or simply to drink in views of the dramatic ochre rock formations jutting from the high

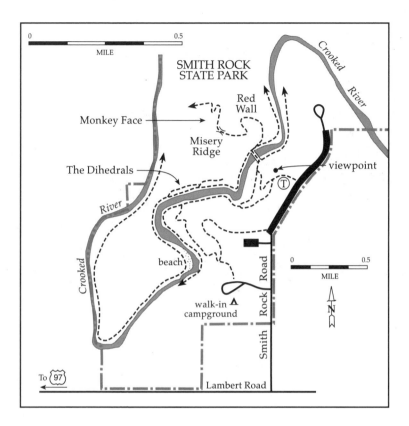

desert. But Smith Rock also offers excellent hiking, from tame paths along the Crooked River to short but taxing ascents. Plan a picnic lunch at a sandy riverside beach, or challenge the kids with a climb to Misery Ridge. In the heat of summer, plan your visit for early or late in the day.

From Bend follow US Highway 97 north 22 miles through Redmond to Terrebonne, and turn east on Smith Rock Road at the sign to Smith Rock State Park. Follow signs 3.2 miles to the park's main day-use area, past the campers' bivouac area (there is no car/RV campground).

From the bluff at the day-use area, asphalt paths lead to a rock-walled viewpoint, then down to a footbridge crossing the Crooked River on either a gradual 0.3-mile trail or a steeper 0.2-mile path. The trail network here is extensive. Following are just two of several options to consider with children.

Smith Rock

RIVER PATH

Cross the footbridge and turn left, with the flow of the river; 0.3 mile from the footbridge look across the river to see Rope de Dope Rock, a favorite spot for beginning climbers. At 0.4 mile a spur route splits off uphill to the Dihedrals climbing area. A few minutes later, look up to the right to the round rock poised in Asterisk Pass. The trail narrows but continues; the sandy beach 0.9 mile from the footbridge makes a good turnaround spot. More energetic hikers could continue around to the base of the famous Monkey Face formation, even following a rough, steep path past Monkey Face to Misery Ridge. From the footbridge a trail leads upriver as well.

MISERY RIDGE

From the footbridge, bear right, then immediately left away from the river toward the formation called the Red Wall. The trail steadily ascends the rock on a series of steps, a rickety wooden staircase, and a footpath. Take it slow and you'll make it all the way to aptly named Misery Ridge, just 0.5 mile but 660 feet from the river. Drop-offs are steep; keep a close eye on children. Return as you came (though more experienced adventurers can manage the alternate return routes down the back side).

For more fun exploring: From Redmond take a 2-mile detour on US Highway 126 east from US Highway 97 to see up close a herd of real reindeer (unless they're out on the road or with Santa himself). Operation Santa Claus welcomes visitors year-round.

69 TUMALO FALLS

Type ▪	Day hike or backpack
Difficulty ▪	Strenuous for children
Distance ▪	6.8 miles, loop
Terrain ▪	Gradual ascent/descent (1100 feet elevation gain)
High point ▪	6040 feet
Hikable ▪	June through October
FYI ▪	Share trail with bikes on first half of loop; no dogs on second half
Contact ▪	Bend/Fort Rock Ranger District, (541) 388-5664

This entire loop would challenge most children, but even brand-new hikers can handle the 0.4-mile round trip to the top of Tumalo Falls. Those with a little more ambition could take on the 2-mile, round-trip hike to Double Falls. The entire loop, passing more and wilder waterfalls and miles of forest, challenges most children, though the ascent is gradual. It's a good choice for older children who like to hike and want to stretch themselves.

From US Highway 97 at Bend, or from downtown Bend, follow signs to Mount Bachelor and Cascade Lakes. A few turns will put you on Galveston Avenue; at the stop sign, go straight on Galveston rather than turning left (toward Cascade Lakes Highway). Drive 10 miles from the stop sign and turn right down gravel Forest Road 4601. Immediately after crossing Tumalo Creek on a single-lane bridge, bear left onto Forest Road 4603 and drive 3.4 miles to Tumalo Falls Picnic Area.

Tumalo Falls, right at the trailhead, is a destination in itself: a wide cataract free-falling onto a rock staircase. Follow signs up North Fork Trail and continue straight where Bridge Creek Trail comes in on the left. At 0.2 mile, the top of the falls, pause to take in the view

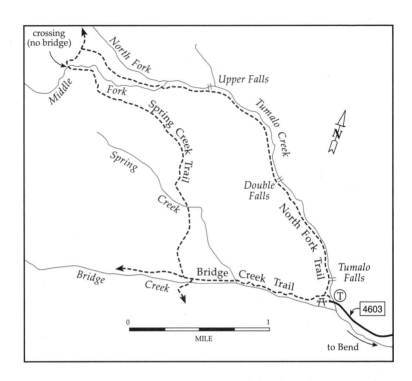

from a platform cantilevered out from the cliffs. The surrounding forest still bears witness to the 1979 Bridge Creek Fire, which burned 4200 acres of old-growth forest. Follow the trail along the fence to return to the main trail.

 Tumalo Creek rushes below you as the trail gently ascends through the pines and firs. At 1 mile you'll see Double Falls, a series of two wide cascades spilling down basalt ledges into a green pool (steep drop-off; take care). Another 0.9 mile leads to Upper Falls, sliding over a steep dome of rock. Just 0.5 mile farther the trail crosses Tumalo Creek's Middle Fork on a narrow bridge—another possible turnaround and/or picnic spot. From here the trail steepens, and as it does, the waterfalls abound. At 3.4 miles you'll reach the junction with Spring Creek Trail; bear left to reach the Middle Fork in another 0.3 mile.

To complete the loop, wade the creek or walk upstream a short distance to cross on a log. The trail resumes across the creek, level, then drops gently to reach a permit station (free at this writing) at the entrance to the City of Bend watershed not quite a mile from the creek crossing. Continue dropping through forest, crossing Spring

Tumalo Falls

Creek, and hiking 1 mile more to the junction with Bridge Creek Trail. At the junction turn left and follow Bridge Creek Trail 1.3 miles alongside stair-stepping Bridge Creek to the junction with the Tumalo Creek Trail just above the parking area.

70 TUMALO MOUNTAIN

Type ▪ Day hike
Difficulty ▪ Very strenuous for children
Distance ▪ 4 miles round trip
Terrain ▪ 1415 feet elevation gain
High point ▪ 7775 feet
Hikable ▪ July through October
Contact ▪ Bend/Fort Rock Ranger District,
(541) 388-5664

What's it like to climb a mountain? Like a very long hike that gets steeper and steeper. The steeper it gets, the slower you go, and the last half-mile can feel like 10 miles. But when you get to the top you feel like you're at the top of the world, and if you've paced yourself right, you're tired—a really good kind of tired.

Tumalo Mountain can give children a taste of that experience in a relatively short outing. The hike begins as a gradual but steady ascent through a forest, then breaks into the open, and steepens radically for the final ascent. At the top, you're clearly not on top of the world: Mount Bachelor is close enough that you'll feel you could hit it with a well-aimed rock, but it's 1290 feet higher. At the top of Tumalo, however, the panorama is grand, with views of Broken Top's crater, the Three Sisters, Sparks Lake, the verdant Tumalo Creek drainage, Bend, and even Smith Rock in the distance. It can be chilly and windy at the top, so carry an extra shirt or windbreaker for lingering on the summit.

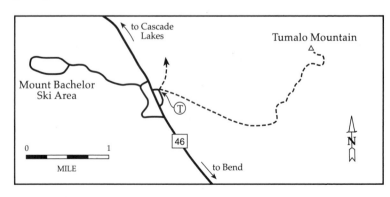

Three Sisters and Broken Top from Tumalo Mountain

From Bend follow Century Drive (which becomes Cascade Lakes Highway and Forest Road 46) about 25 miles to the Mount Bachelor ski area. Just past the first Mount Bachelor turnoff (3 miles west of the Sunriver cutoff road), turn right at the sign to the Tumalo Mountain trailhead parking area. In winter, this is a large snow-park area.

The trail begins at the east end of the parking area and winds uphill, alternating between forest and meadow. Peek through the trees to see the ski runs on Mount Bachelor. Note how contorted some of the trees are, a result of being under snow more than half the year.

For the final 0.5 mile the forest falls away and you walk straight up the steep trail to the summit. This is a good place to teach children the "wedding march" style of hiking, emulating climbers, as an alternative to the hike-rest-hike-rest style that kids can fall into. When you do stop to rest, kids who ski in winter will enjoy seeing Mount Bachelor's snow-free runs so clearly etched among the trees. On the return hike, they may wish they had ski poles to help them schuss down the steep summit trail.

For more fun exploring: Take a series of two high-speed quad chair lifts to the top of Mount Bachelor (fee charged) for a look back at Tumalo Mountain; ride or walk the 3 miles back to Sunrise Lodge on informal dirt trails and paths.

71 TODD LAKE

Type ▪ Day hike
Difficulty ▪ Easy for children
Distance ▪ 2.4 miles, loop
Terrain ▪ Nearly level
High point ▪ 6150 feet
Hikable ▪ July through October
Contact ▪ Bend/Fort Rock Ranger District,
(541) 388-5664

The southern end of picturesque, 45-acre Todd Lake is just 0.2 mile from the trailhead parking area, making it a popular spot for camping on late-summer weekends. That accessibility also makes it appealing for an easy, level hike. Count on mosquitoes early in the season; all season wear boots (or expect soggy sneakers) for walking around the lake's marshy far end.

From Bend follow Century Drive (which becomes Cascade Lakes Highway and Forest Road 46) about 25 miles toward the Mount Bachelor ski area. About 1.5 miles past Mount Bachelor, turn right at the sign to Todd Lake and drive 0.5 mile to the parking area above the meadow. Begin hiking up the gated road marked with a campground sign.

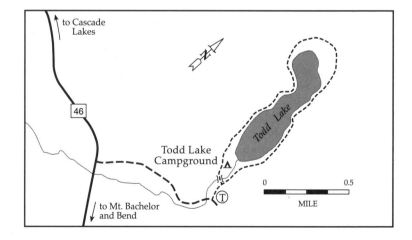

A short distance from the parking area the road splits; you can go in either direction to circle Todd Lake. Going clockwise, cross the lake's outlet to reach a small campground on the lakeshore; Broken Top can be seen rising beyond the water. Walk to the lake edge and pick up the trail, which closely follows the shore.

Wildflowers border the trail here and there; occasionally you'll step over wet spots where springs are seeping into the lake. Approaching the lake's far end, cross rivulets that zigzag across a widening meadow. The trail per se disappears at the far end, where the terrain gets soggy. Pick a route to stay as dry as possible.

Pick up the trail where the marsh gives way to drier ground. The trail then reenters the forest, following close to the lake's east shore for the walk back to the junction.

Todd Lake

72 LAVA RIVER CAVE

Type ■ Day hike
Difficulty ■ Easy for children
Distance ■ 2.4 miles round trip
Terrain ■ Gradual (200 feet elevation gain)
High point ■ 4500 feet
Hikable ■ Early May through mid-October
Contact ■ Bend/Fort Rock Ranger District, (541) 388-5664, or Lava Lands Visitor Center, (541) 593-2421 (April through October)

Hiking in a cave? It's quite possible—and enticing to children—when the cave is a mile-long uncollapsed lava tube. The cave is part of Newberry National Volcanic Monument. The Forest Service opens the cave to visitors during the summer, charging a small fee for admission (children under 12 free) and another nominal fee for lantern rental. Take a flashlight for back-up light, but rent a lantern as well; you can see much more than with a flashlight, and responsible children can take turns holding the light. Be sure to wear warm clothes as well; regardless of the temperature outside, the cave is always about 40 degrees Fahrenheit.

Children will be awed by the whole experience: the darkness broken by the lanterns' light and the long shadows they cast, the eerie sounds of hissing lanterns and echoing voices, and just the knowledge that they're under the earth, out of touch with familiar landmarks. Some young children may find it too frightening. Adventurous types may need reminders not to wander too far from the light; it's easy to twist an ankle wandering alone in the dark. Rest assured there are no side chambers to mistakenly wander into.

 From Bend take US Highway 97 south about 14 miles and turn east at the sign to Lava River Cave. Pick up a free trail brochure at the entrance booth for interpretation along the way or for reading after the hike.

You enter the lava tube at a point where the roof collapsed thousands of years ago. Look back to see that the tube actually continues in the other direction (but is currently blocked off). Stairs lead down into the cave; once on the cave floor, begin a slow descent on a rock and sand surface with a few stairs here and there. About 0.25 mile from the entrance, the lava tube crosses under the highway (don't bother listening for cars; they're a good 80 feet above you). Then at about 0.6 mile look for the Sand Garden, where dripping water has created a fantastical landscape in a field of sand that, over centuries, has slowly entered the cave. The hike through the tube ends after 1.2 miles, where sand blocks further progress.

Like other lava tubes, Lava River Cave was formed when a flow of hot lava from Newberry Volcano began to cool and crusted over. The lava inside the flow drained out, leaving an empty tube. The "river" refers to the river of lava; geologists believe no river of water ever flowed in the cave.

For more fun exploring: Visit Lava Lands Visitor Center, 1 mile north of Lava River Cave, for information on the 0.9-mile paved loop trail at Lava Cast Forest and other Newberry National Volcanic Monument points of interest.

Volcanic rock, Lava Cast Forest

73 PAULINA CREEK

Type ■ Day hike

Hikable ■ June through October (longer season at lower end)

Contact ■ Bend/Fort Rock Ranger District, (541) 388-5664, or Lava Lands Visitor Center, (541) 593-2421 (April through October)

PAULINA CREEK FALLS

Difficulty ■ Easy for children

Distance ■ 0.2 to 1 mile round trip

Terrain ■ Up to 300 feet elevation gain

High point ■ 6330 feet

PAULINA CREEK TRAIL, LOWER SECTION

Difficulty ■ Easy to moderate for children

Distance ■ 2.75 miles one way

Terrain ■ Steady ascent (420 feet elevation gain)

High point ■ 4720 feet

FYI ■ Share trail with bicycles (bicycles allowed to ascend only)

PAULINA CREEK TRAIL, UPPER SECTION

Difficulty ■ Strenuous for children

Distance ■ 5.75 miles one way

Terrain ■ Steady ascent (1610 feet elevation gain)

High point ■ 6330 feet

FYI ■ Share trail with bicycles (bicycles allowed to ascend only)

The 8.5-mile Peter Skene Ogden Trail following Paulina Creek from Paulina Lake, at Newberry Caldera, down the volcano's pine-forested slope offers waterfalls, wading, and pleasant creekside hiking. The trip can be hot and dusty midday in midsummer; go early or late in the day. Better yet, try it in late spring, when the waterfalls are gushing, or autumn, when aspen leaves flutter gold against the red ponderosa pines. For a short outing, walk to views of 100-foot Paulina Creek Falls along the north or south side of the creek.

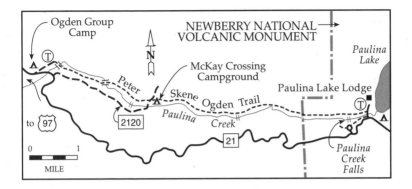

PAULINA CREEK FALLS

About 20 miles south of Bend on US Highway 97, turn east on Forest Road 21 at the sign to Newberry Caldera and continue 12.2 miles to the Paulina Creek Falls Picnic Area. From the trailhead at the parking area, bear right to the main falls viewpoint in a short distance, or bear left to switchback down 0.2 mile to a viewing platform at the base of the falls. Alternatively, drive 0.3 mile farther and turn left toward Paulina Lake Lodge, parking near the lake's outlet (the start of Paulina Creek). A woodsy trail leads 0.3 mile down the south side of the creek past the viewpoint to the picnic area parking lot. Or, from the lake, cross the creek and take Peter Skene Ogden Trail down the north side of the creek 0.3 mile to a view of the falls from the other side.

PAULINA CREEK TRAIL

Road access at McKay Crossing Campground splits the 8.5-mile trail into two sections. A round-trip hike from the bottom (at Ogden Group Camp) up to the trail's end at Paulina Lake would exceed most adults' capacity, let alone kids'. But either section, hiked round-trip, could make a pleasant outing. Best of all, leave a shuttle car at the top (at Paulina Lake) and hike the entire trail one way, downhill. With its gentle grade and proximity to US 97, the lower section is the best choice for a moderately easy round-trip hike (no lake views, though).

About 20 miles south of Bend on US 97, turn east on Forest Road 21 at the sign to Newberry Caldera. Go 2.8 miles and turn left at the sign for Ogden Group Camp, then follow signs 0.3 mile to the trailhead. To reach McKay Crossing by car, continue up Road 21 another 0.5 mile, turn left onto Forest Road 2120 at the sign to McKay

Paulina Creek near Ogden Group Camp

Crossing Campground, and follow the road 2.3 miles to the campground. The trail starts on a rise just across the creek. The upper trailhead is by Paulina Lake Lodge, 12.5 miles up Road 21 from US 97. You can leave your car in a wide parking area south of the boat dock or in a picnic area just up Road 21.

Lower Section

From the lower trailhead at Ogden Group Camp, walk up some steps, then walk about 50 yards to a sturdy pole footbridge crossing Paulina Creek. The trail heads up the creek's south bank, following it closely most of the way to another bridge at 0.9 mile. This is a good spot to picnic or dip toes; the creek is fairly shallow and safe. From the bridge, the trail steepens a bit, but not much. It veers away from the creek much of the way to McKay Crossing—always in earshot, but not always in view—passing through a forest of lodgepole and ponderosa pines. About 0.25 mile short of McKay Crossing, the creek cascades into a rocky gorge. You have to walk off the trail a few steps for a good view, but take care in doing so. This is a good turnaround if you're hiking back the way you came—the campground just ahead is uninteresting, but the creek does flatten out there, for those in need of a refreshing wade. (There's also an outhouse, but no drinking water.) The final 0.25 mile of this lower trail section swings away from the creek, passes the campground, and leads to the McKay Crossing.

Upper Section

The hike east and up from McKay Crossing closely follows the creek and is steeper—which means you'll see more waterfalls along the way. About 0.3 mile before the trail's end at Paulina Lake you'll reach a view of Paulina Creek Falls. The trail emerges next to the bridge on the short access road from Road 21 to Paulina Lake Lodge.

74 PAULINA LAKE

Type ■	Day hike or backpack
Difficulty ■	Strenuous for children (easy to beach)
Distance ■	7.5 miles, loop (2.5 miles round trip to beach)
Terrain ■	Nearly level (195 feet elevation gain)
High point ■	195 feet
Hikable ■	June through October
Contact ■	Bend/Fort Rock Ranger District, (541) 388-5664, or Lava Lands Visitor Center, (541) 593-2421 (April through October)

Why walk around a lake that's accessible by car? In the case of Paulina Lake, three reasons come to mind: to get to some otherwise inaccessible parts of the shoreline, to see the lake and surrounding country from a different perspective, and, perhaps most of all, to get the sense of accomplishment that accompanies such a trek. Though motorboats slowly trolling on the lake keep you from feeling "away from it all," the lake attracts more anglers than hikers, and you're likely to be alone on much of the trail. This hike is recommended for older children who enjoy a challenge. For a shorter, one-way hike (4 miles), leave a shuttle car at Little Crater Campground. For an even shorter hike, just walk down to the beach and back.

About 20 miles south of Bend on US Highway 97, turn east on Forest Road 21 at the sign to Newberry Caldera. Follow it 12.5 miles to the caldera rim and turn left toward Paulina Lake Campground. Park at the boat dock past the campground.

To walk clockwise, head toward Paulina Lake Lodge along the shore to a trail sign and the beginning of a footpath. The trail reaches a nice gravel beach and campsite (with outhouse) and view of Paulina

Paulina Lake

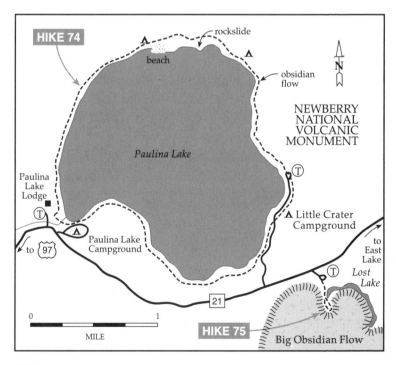

Peak at about 1.25 miles. At 2 miles the trail leads away from the lake and up the hill (the only significant ascent on the trail) to avoid a steep, red rockslide along the lake.

Back down near lake level, notice the way the trail sparkles with tiny chips of obsidian; they're from an obsidian flow a few minutes ahead on the trail. The shoreline grows rockier here, more dramatic, on the approach to Little Crater Campground, at 4 miles.

Walk through the campground on the road for about 0.5 mile until the trail resumes along the now sandy lakeshore. Pass in front of some privately owned summer homes and into a wide, grassy marsh teeming with butterflies and dragonflies. The trail reenters forest, crosses creeks on little footbridges, and emerges at Paulina Lake Campground.

75 OBSIDIAN FLOW

Type ▪	Day hike
Difficulty ▪	Easy for children
Distance ▪	0.7 mile, loop
Terrain ▪	Slight ascent (100 feet elevation gain)
High point ▪	6600 feet
Hikable ▪	June through October
Contact ▪	Bend/Fort Rock Ranger District, (541) 388-5664, or Lava Lands Visitor Center, (541) 593-2421 (April through October)

Though this trail is too short to qualify as a genuine hike—it's really a little interpretive trail—make a point of walking it on a visit to Newberry Caldera. Even in the volcanic Oregon Cascades, it's unlikely you'll see another mountain of black, glasslike obsidian. It's fascinating, and it offers an opportunity to talk about how glass is made from silica—a process similar to the way this obsidian was made deep inside the now-dormant volcano. A paved trail leads safely up onto the flow. Keep the kids on the trail; off-trail, the obsidian is literally as slick and sharp as glass.

About 20 miles south of Bend on US Highway 97, turn east on Forest Road 21 at the sign to Newberry Caldera. Follow it 12.5 miles to the caldera rim, then continue on the main road 2.3 miles to the sign for "Obsidian Flow," at the trailhead parking area.

Obsidian Flow

The path threads among lodgepole pines to a staircase that leads up and onto the obsidian flow; look over your left shoulder to see aptly named Lost Lake. Cross a chasm on a sturdy footbridge, then turn right or left to make the loop. Short spur trails lead to benches and viewpoints. From the highest point there's a magnificent view not only of the obsidian flow surrounding you but also of Paulina Peak, Paulina Lake, and Mt. Bachelor, South Sister, and the tip of Middle Sister.

The obsidian flow was formed an estimated 1300 years ago during an eruption of the caldera between Paulina and East Lakes, Central Oregon's most recent volcanic eruption. The rock under the caldera was rich in silica, the main ingredient in glass; when it melted from the heat of the earth, and later cooled, obsidian was formed. Notice the few scraggy pines that have managed to grow seemingly out of bare rock—but really in niches where water and a little soil have accumulated over the centuries. Tempting as it may be, don't pocket any obsidian souvenirs, leaving less for others to enjoy. (Besides, it's against the law.)

Ecola State Park

THE COAST

76 TILLAMOOK HEAD

Type ■ Day hike or backpack
Difficulty ■ Strenuous for children
Distance ■ 6 miles one way
Terrain ■ Steady to steep ascents (900 feet elevation gain)
High point ■ 1150 feet
Hikable ■ Year-round
Contact ■ Ecola State Park, (503) 436-2844

The north side of Tillamook Head is steep, the trail challenging to young legs. Although the south side is a little gentler, it's still a steady uphill climb on a sometimes muddy path. What's the appeal? History—you're walking in the footsteps of the Lewis and Clark expedition. Views—you'll see the ocean falling away below and the old lighthouse off the headland. Satisfaction— you've made it to the top. With a shuttle car you can walk from one end to the other, but most people choose one end to start and walk round trip to a viewpoint atop the head.

To reach the northern trailhead from the junction of US Highways 26 and 101, take US Highway 101 north 2.7 miles to Seaside and turn left at the first signal, on Avenue U. Drive 0.2 mile, turn left onto South Edgewood Road, and continue 1.2 miles. South Edgewood Road becomes Sunset Boulevard, passes a golf course, and leads to the trailhead at the end of the paved road. To reach the southern trailhead from the junction of US Highways 26 and 101, travel south 3 miles on US 101 and take the first Cannon Beach exit. Follow the road down the hill and turn right at the sign to Ecola State Park. Follow signs to the park 3.7 miles, passing Ecola Point, to parking at Indian Beach.

From the northern trailhead, pick up the trail at the southeast end of the parking area. The toughest part of the hike is the first 1.5 miles, as the trail switchbacks up about 700 feet onto Tillamook Head. At 1 mile there's a good view to the north of Seaside and, beyond it, Cape Disappointment across the Columbia River. Continue another 0.5 mile, bearing right at a junction, where the trail levels out.

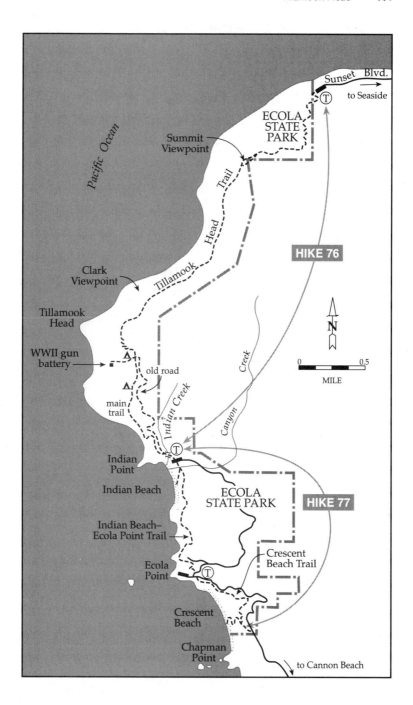

Pacific Ocean

ECOLA STATE PARK

Sunset Blvd.

(T) to Seaside

Summit Viewpoint

Tillamook Head Trail

HIKE 76

Clark Viewpoint

Tillamook Head

WWII gun battery

old road

main trail

Indian Creek

Canyon Creek

N

0   0.5
MILE

Indian Point

Indian Beach

(T)

ECOLA STATE PARK

HIKE 77

Indian Beach–Ecola Point Trail

Crescent Beach Trail

Ecola Point

(T)

Crescent Beach

Chapman Point

to Cannon Beach

Backpackers on Tillamook Head

Roll along through deep forest 3.7 miles, where a plaque announces Clarks Viewpoint. In January 1806 Captain William Clark used virtually this same trail to walk from Fort Clatsop near Astoria to Cannon Beach to investigate reports of a beached whale there.

From the viewpoint the trail drops a bit, then reaches a campsite with an outhouse at an old road crossing at 4.4 miles. Follow the road west 0.2 mile to see the ruins of a World War II gun battery, nearly obscured by vegetation; it was built as part of a series of coastal defense fortifications. Near the outhouse, look for a huge stump with springboard notches cut by early-day loggers. At the junction continue straight south to follow the trail down to Indian Beach. The trail leads uphill a bit, then levels out and starts dropping. Look around the forest here for nurse logs and for big stumps, leftover from old logging operations. At 4.8 miles the trail passes a small, level clearing that makes a nice campsite. Then the trail drops down along Indian Creek, crosses it on a footbridge, and ends at Indian Beach.

Alternately, at the junction at 4.4 miles, bear east at the sign to Indian Creek; the old road it follows veers south, ending at Indian Beach.

For more fun exploring: Time your trip to coincide with low tide and you'll discover some treasures—to look at, not to pick up or take home—in the tide pools at Indian Beach.

77 ECOLA POINT

Type ▪ Day hike
Hikable ▪ Year-round
Contact ▪ Ecola State Park, (503) 436-2844

ECOLA POINT–INDIAN BEACH
Difficulty ▪ Easy for children
Distance ▪ 3 miles round trip
Terrain ▪ Rolling (140 feet elevation gain)
High point ▪ 190 feet

CRESCENT BEACH
Difficulty ▪ Easy to moderate for children
Distance ▪ 2.4 miles round trip
Terrain ▪ Level, with steady ascents (250 feet elevation gain)
High point ▪ 250 feet

The path between Ecola and Indian Points leads above a rocky and dramatic stretch of coastline accessible only to hikers. It's a fun, easy hike—one way, or round trip—for families vacationing in Cannon Beach. Extend the hike south from Ecola Point to catch the trail down to hidden Crescent Beach.

From the Seaside junction of US Highways 26 and 101, travel 3 miles south on US 101 and take the first Cannon Beach exit. Follow the road down the hill and turn right at the sign to Ecola State Park. Follow park signs 2 miles to parking at Ecola Point. Start here, or return to the main road and continue another 1.7 miles to park at Indian Beach, where you can walk north to south (putting the wind at your back in summer).

Stormy day at Ecola State Park

ECOLA POINT–INDIAN BEACH

From the Indian Beach parking lot, follow the sign to the ocean beach. Cross Canyon Creek, then bear left at the fork, rather than right to the beach. The trail alternates between woodsy path and shoreline vista trail as it gradually ascends along the bluff above the sea. At about 0.5 mile the trail reaches a rather steep slide area. At 0.8 mile the trail crosses an open slope with flowers in the spring, a good spot to rest and watch for fishing boats in summer. The trail emerges from the woods at the edge of the Ecola Point parking area at 3 miles.

CRESCENT BEACH

To find Crescent Beach, pick up the trail at the southeast corner of the parking lot at Ecola Point, near the rest rooms. After climbing some stairs you'll reach the park road; follow it for a few paces until the trail resumes, heading down the bank to the west. It rolls through ancient forest (muddy in places), crossing a creek on a footbridge at about 0.5 mile. At 1 mile you'll reach a junction: Here you will turn right; switchback down the steep, forested hillside; cross another little bridge; and come to the beach. Return as you came.

78 ARCH CAPE

Type ■ Day hike
Difficulty ■ Easy to moderate for children
Distance ■ 1.75 miles one way
Terrain ■ Gentle ascent (320 feet elevation gain)
High point ■ 320 feet
Hikable ■ Year-round
Contact ■ Nehalem Bay State Park, (503) 368-5154

The woods blanketing Arch Cape are deep, the summer sunlight filtered through layers of Douglas fir and cedar. This hike is a good introduction to old-growth forests. But there's another reason why it's in this book. There's a small school at Cape Falcon that some children from Cannon Beach attend. One recent winter the tunnel at Arch Cape was closed for several months for reconstruction. So kids

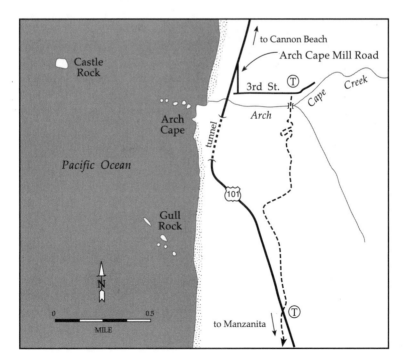

Suspension bridge over Necarney Creek

living on the north side of the cape walked this trail to help get to and from school! Arrange to walk it one way, with a pickup along the highway at the south end, or just wander south from Arch Cape as far as you like, returning as you came. The trail continues south to Cape Falcon and eventually to Neahkahnie Mountain.

 From Cannon Beach take US Highway 101 south to Arch Cape and turn east onto Arch Cape Mill Road (a short distance north of the tunnel). Turn left to follow the road, which turns into Third Street. The trail, marked by a post, starts at the south end of Third Street. (If you're leaving a car here, note that it's a residential neighborhood, so choose your parking spot with care.) The trail begins with a suspension footbridge over Arch Cape Creek next to its confluence with a cascading side stream. Follow the trail up about 0.1 mile, turning right at the trail post pointing toward Cape Falcon.

The trail leads around the back of Arch Cape, away from the ocean, climbing gradually through a lovely climax forest. At about 1 mile the sight and sound of the ocean return; shortly the trail turns onto an old road and begins a descent toward US 101, hitting the highway at about 1.75 miles. (By car, look for the old road on the east side of the highway 0.75 mile south of the tunnel.)

For more fun exploring: Consider a stop at Hug Point State Park, 1.75 miles north of Arch Cape. Follow the beach a short distance north, around a low point of land, to see, at low or midtide, where a road was cut into the rock early in the 1900s to allow cars to round the point, long before the coast highway was built.

79 CAPE FALCON

Type ▪	Day hike
Difficulty ▪	Moderate for children
Distance ▪	5 miles round trip
Terrain ▪	Rolling grade (300 feet elevation gain)
High point ▪	240 feet
Hikable ▪	Year-round
Contact ▪	Nehalem Bay State Park, (503) 368-5154

The hike out to Cape Falcon leads through a wonderful coastal forest with all its delights: birds twittering, shafts of sunlight playing through the lacy conifer branches, and trickling creeks. At the end, follow a narrow corridor onto the grassy, brushy, but treeless cape, where children can follow mazes in the salal and watch for whales and fishing boats offshore.

From Cannon Beach take US Highway 101 south 10 miles and turn right into the first (the northernmost) of three parking areas for Oswald West State Park.

You could actually begin at any of the parking areas; a maze of loop trails winds through the forest here. The simplest approach is to pick up the trail leading west from the northernmost parking lot. The trail winds through an inspiring forest above Short Sand Creek, roaring to its meeting with the Pacific. At about 0.5 mile turn right at the trail junction. Soon the trail crosses a small creek and, at 1 mile, enters an old logged-off blowdown area. Just past the blowdown area,

Neahkahnie Mountain from Cape Falcon Trail

you will see—still standing—the kinds of trees that had blown down: huge spruce, hemlock, and Douglas fir.

The trail continues to roll along, crossing small creeks. On a sunny day you will see the ocean sparkling through the trees. At about 1.8 miles the trail enters a clearing, granting views south to Short Sand Beach and Neahkahnie Mountain. At 2 miles, after a climb up a couple of short switchbacks, there's an even better view. Continue following the contours of the hill on the mostly level path to a junction, unsigned, with a spur trail leading west onto the top of Cape Falcon. Follow it 0.2 mile, through a virtual tunnel of salal at first, onto the treeless, windswept cape tip—a dramatic spot. It's not particularly hazardous as long as children use reasonable care, but the cliffs are steep. Return as you came. The trail, part of the long-distance Oregon Coast Trail, continues north to Arch Cape.

For more fun exploring: Visit Short Sand Beach, following signs south and west about 0.5 mile from your parking spot at Oswald West State Park, to wade, picnic, dig, or watch the surfers.

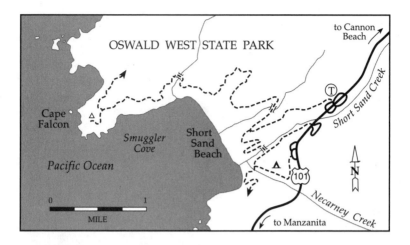

80 NEAHKAHNIE MOUNTAIN

Type ▪ Day hike
Difficulty ▪ Moderate to strenuous for children
Distance ▪ 3 miles round trip
Terrain ▪ Steady ascent (890 feet elevation gain)
High point ▪ 1631 feet
Hikable ▪ Year-round
Contact ▪ Nehalem Bay State Park, (503) 368-5154

Legend has it that somewhere on Neahkahnie Mountain a treasure trove 200-plus years old lies buried, waiting to be discovered. Whether or not it's true, it's a great source of speculation on a trek to the summit of this looming north coast landmark. The easiest way up is from the south, though a trail leads to the summit from the northwest as well.

From Manzanita drive north on US Highway 101 for 1.5 miles to a hiker sign, turn east on a rough gravel access road, and continue 0.5 mile to the trailhead. There is room for several cars to park. Southbound, the access road is about 13 miles from Cannon Beach.

The trail ascends steadily, switchbacking up the hillside in and out of gloomy Sitka spruce stands and open hillsides thick with salal and salmonberry or, in spring, such wildflowers as the sky-pink coast fawn lily. The fourth switchback (0.5 mile from the trailhead) offers the

Sitka spruce tunnel on Neahkahnie Mountain Trail

first of many great views. Even kids love the view because of the recognizable landmarks, including US 101, the Nehalem River and Bay, and the towns of Nehalem and Wheeler.

Continue climbing the mountain's south side, up more than a dozen switchbacks, to a wooden trail marker post at the summit ridge (1.2 miles). Bear left up the forest road to a collection of radio and

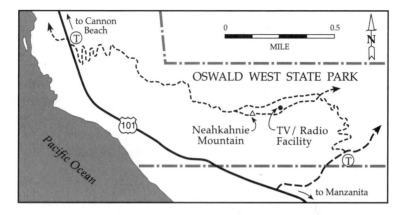

TV antennas at a cement-block building. Round the building on a rough trail and continue a few steps through the woods to the tiny, knobby summit. It's a great perch for a picnic on a sunny day. Children must take care in climbing around the steep hillside. Return as you came.

With a shuttle car you have another option. You can continue west and north down the mountain through 4.5 miles of gorgeous forest to the mountain's northern trailhead, on US 101 about 1.5 miles north of where the southern trailhead access road leaves the highway (and about 1 mile south of the southernmost parking area at Oswald West State Park).

81 CAPE LOOKOUT

Type:	▪ Day hike
Difficulty	▪ Moderate for children
Distance	▪ 5 miles round trip
Terrain	▪ Rolling, gentle ascent (500 feet elevation gain)
High point	▪ 850 feet
Hikable	▪ Year-round
Contact	▪ Cape Lookout State Park, (503) 842-4981

The great appeal of a hike to the tip of Cape Lookout is the chance to spot whales—motivation enough for some children. Cape Lookout

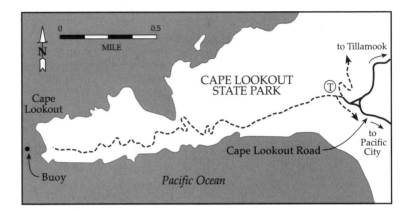

is one of the best whale-watching sites on the Oregon Coast, and with more than two hundred gray whales now summering off Oregon, the chances of spotting a whale in midsummer aren't bad. Unfortunately, the best times are when the trail is at its muddiest: mid-March, during the northward migration, and December through early January, when the migrants are headed south to Baja for the winter. At those times, an average of fifteen to thirty whales may pass by in an hour.

Even if whales aren't sighted, the hike itself is worthwhile. Take it slow and easy, enjoying the views and the forest along the way. After the hike, drive south to Pacific City and look north at the long headland sticking way out from the mainland to see what you have just accomplished.

From Tillamook follow signs west and south about 10 miles to the entrance to Cape Lookout State Park and campground. Rather than turning here, however, continue another 2.8 miles on Cape Lookout Road to a trailhead parking area on the right. From Pacific City follow Three Capes Scenic Route north about 13 miles to the trailhead.

Two trails start side by side at the west end of the parking area. The trail on the right leads north 2.5 miles to the park's campground. Instead, take the left-hand trail. In about 75 yards go straight where another trail comes in from the left (it leads 2 miles down to the beach).

The terrain that the trail follows to the cape tip is rolling, but mostly slowly descending. At 0.6 mile the forest opens up to grand views of the beach and headlands to the south. From here, watch on the right for a plaque memorializing the victims of a 1943 plane crash. At 1.2 miles—about the halfway point—the trail reaches a fenced cliff on the north side of the cape, granting views of Oceanside and Three Arch Rocks.

The route winds back to the cape's south side, teasing hikers on with occasional views. A single strand of wire cable strung along the cliff does little more than warn hikers to take care; children may not get the hint, so watch them here. While approaching the tip, kids can listen for the buoy anchored offshore, moaning with the rhythm of the swells. Once they spot it, it's just a few more minutes' walk to the rocky point at the trail's end. Carry a picnic and binoculars and plan to linger awhile if you want to spot any whales, as the whales travel on their own schedule. Return as you came.

Cape Lookout

82 HARTS COVE

Type ▪	Day hike or backpack
Difficulty ▪	Moderate to strenuous for children
Distance ▪	5.8 miles round trip
Terrain ▪	Rolling, with steady ascent (800 feet elevation gain)
High point ▪	960 feet
Hikable ▪	July 17 to December 31
Contact ▪	Hebo Ranger District, (503) 392-3161

The hike to Harts Cove is more like a mountain hike than a beach hike, traversing as it does deep forest and offering only occasional,

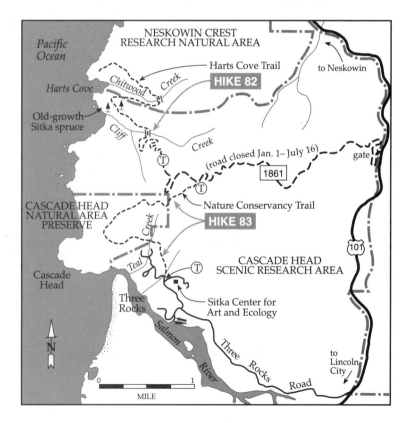

Harts Cove

distant ocean views. The hike doesn't go up a high headland or down to a secluded beach, but leads to a grassy slope overlooking a dramatic and remote stretch of coastline. On the way the trail winds through a magnificent hemlock and Sitka spruce forest and crosses a couple of rushing streams on footbridges. Most of the elevation loss (and on the return, gain) is in the first mile; after that, it's a pleasant stroll.

From Neskowin take US Highway 101 south 3.6 miles and turn right on Cascade Head Road (Forest Road 1861), which is 4 miles south of State Highway 18. (The road is gated from January 1 through July 16 to keep hikers off the trail during nesting season.) Follow Road 1861 west for 4.1 miles to the trailhead at road's end and park.

The trail drops quickly, steeply at times, switchbacking down the hill until it reaches a footbridge across Cliff Creek at 1 mile. Cross the creek, its bank lush with wildflowers in the spring. From here the trail climbs gently; listen for the sounds of birds and the rush of the creek, slowly fading. At about 1.5 miles you will hear the crash of waves on the cliffs below; beginning in October, the loud barking of California sea lions fills the air as well.

Shortly a sign announces the Neskowin Crest Research Area and suggests looking around at the remains of 250-year-old Sitka spruce that have survived fires that destroyed other trees in the forest. Just beyond the sign is a bench offering the first view of Harts Cove. The cove looks so close—but it's still a good mile away by trail. Follow the trail back up a ravine, across Chitwood Creek, then back through the loveliest, quietest, most magnificent old-growth forest yet seen along the trail. At 2.7 miles the trail emerges from the forest near the top of the grassy slope that overlooks Harts Cove to the south. Walk down the slope another 0.2 mile to peek down at the cove. There's a lot of room to play and explore without getting too close to the cliffs, but adults will want to watch children carefully just the same. There is no access down to (or, more to the point, back out of) Harts Cove. Return as you came.

83 CASCADE HEAD

Type ▪	Day hike
Difficulty ▪	Moderate for children
Distance ▪	3.6 miles round trip
Terrain ▪	Gentle ascent (210 feet elevation gain)
High point ▪	330 feet
Hikable ▪	Year-round
FYI ▪	No dogs allowed
Contact ▪	The Nature Conservancy, (503) 230-1221

The hike to the grassy tip of Cascade Head traverses lovely woods and crosses boisterous creeks. But it's the view at the end—of the

Salmon River estuary and coastline to the south—that makes this hike so memorable. A visit late or early in the day may reward hikers with views of deer grazing on the headland's open slopes.

The most popular trail on Cascade Head is the southern route to the headland's tip. From US Highway 101 (1.3 miles north of State Highway 18) turn west onto Three Rocks Road and drive about 2.5 miles to a fork at the county boat ramp. Bear right, up the hill, and continue 0.5 mile to the trailhead on the right, just past the entrance to Sitka Center for Art and Ecology. Roadside parking is limited.

The trail starts up a steep hillside for the first 0.5 mile, then levels off, crossing several small creeks on wooden footbridges and board-walks. Gently ascending, the trail follows the hillside's contours through the forest, emerging onto the open prairie a short walk from the south viewpoint, near a line of fencing beyond which hiking is prohibited. Return as you came, unless you're in the mood for some anaerobic exercise in the form of a steep climb to the summit knoll, another 0.7 mile and 880 feet straight up. The trail continues an-other mile to the north trailhead (3.5 miles one way), accessible from Forest Road 1861 mid-July through December (see Hike 82).

Mouth of the Salmon River, from Cascade Head

The trail out to Cascade Head passes through a 300-acre preserve owned and managed by The Nature Conservancy since 1966. Though the preserve is open to the public, the conservancy is rightfully protective of this seaside gem. Be extra careful to leave no trace here. In addition to using ordinary trail etiquette (don't litter, don't pick any vegetation), leave your dog at home and walk only on the trail. Certainly don't camp or build a fire on the headland.

84 DRIFT CREEK FALLS

Type	Day hike
Difficulty	Moderate for children
Distance	3 miles round trip
Terrain	Gentle ascent; steep from creek (380 feet elevation gain)
High point	910 feet
Hikable	Year-round
Contact	Hebo Ranger District, (503) 392-3161

It's named for the waterfall, and it's dramatic enough: an unnamed tributary pours over a mossy cliff and free-falls 75 feet onto a pool in Drift Creek. But it's the suspension bridge near the trail's end that

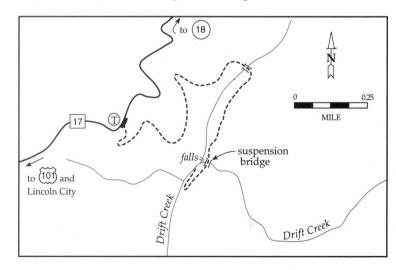

Drift Creek Falls and suspension bridge

catches the most attention on this hike. It hangs between support towers, each 29 feet tall, and is anchored to the bedrock on either side of Drift Creek. From the middle of the bridge you get a good look at the falls—if you dare; its gentle swaying motion can be a bit unnerving. It's a great hike for children with self-control and a well-developed sense of adventure—not for daredevils.

From US Highway 101 at the south end of Lincoln City, turn east onto Drift Creek Road, then south onto South Drift Creek Road. Turn east onto Forest Road 17 and continue for 10 miles to the roadside trailhead. Alternately, from State Highway 18 at Rose Lodge, turn south onto Bear Creek Road (which becomes Forest Road 17) and follow signs about 9 miles.

The hike to the falls descends gently, mainly through former clearcuts now growing trees ranging from 10 to 50 years old, plus a narrow band of old growth. At 1 mile a small footbridge crosses the unnamed creek the falls is on; at 1.25 miles the trail reaches the suspension bridge overlooking the falls. To reach the trail's end, cross the bridge and follow the trail's switchbacks down 0.25 mile, dropping 100 feet in elevation to the creek's edge. Return as you came.

85 MIKE MILLER PARK

Type ▪ Day hike
Difficulty ▪ Easy for children
Distance ▪ 1 mile loop
Terrain ▪ Gentle ascent (120 feet elevation gain)
High point ▪ 150 feet
Hikable ▪ Year-round
Contact ▪ Lincoln County Parks, (541) 265-5747

Just off US Highway 101 south of Newport there's a short loop trail designed to introduce school children to a variety of coastal forest habitats—including old growth, with huge stumps from long-ago logging—and blowdown. The public is welcome on Mike Miller Park Educational Trail as well.

 Look for a trail sign on the east side of US Highway 101 just north of the entrance (on the west side) to South Beach State Park, about 1.2 miles south of Yaquina Bay Bridge. The gravel road to the trail

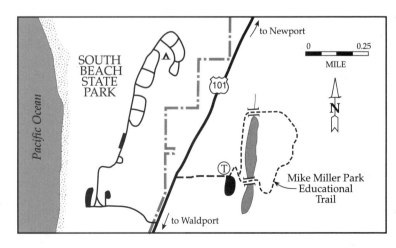

goes straight a short distance and then swings right into a large parking area. Park and walk back to the trailhead, located where the road curves. Follow the trail uphill a short distance to where it splits into a loop; bearing left, the trail follows an old railroad bed for about 0.2 mile. It then veers right, drops down to cross the end of a long lake on a wooden boardwalk, and begins climbing through a Sitka spruce forest.

The trail continues to climb slowly until it reaches the ridge top, from which it slowly drops down to the edge of a blowdown area alongside a clearcut at about 0.7 mile. It then drops down to a long footbridge across the other end of the lake and completes the loop.

Footbridge and overlook platform at Mike Miller Park

For more fun exploring: The trail is just across US 101 from South Beach State Park, with its beach access, campground, and paved trail through the dunes. Use the paved trail to bike to the Oregon Coast Aquarium and Hatfield Marine Science Center. Between the aquarium and the science center is a 0.5-mile footpath along Yaquina Bay and across a finger of the bay via a long wooden boardwalk.

86 YACHATS 804 TRAIL

Type ■	Day hike
Difficulty ■	Easy for children
Distance ■	1.5 miles round trip
Terrain ■	Nearly level
High point ■	10 feet
Hikable ■	Year-round
Contact ■	Beachside State Recreation Site, (541) 563-3220

The 804 Trail is an old road right-of-way that's been reclaimed for pedestrians as part of the Oregon Coast Trail. It starts in a state park wayside, passes between private homes and motels to the east and a stretch of wave-sculpted rock and pocket beaches, then leads to the beach. At high tide the water show here is fantastic, as incoming waves smash into narrow chutes and shoot into the air.

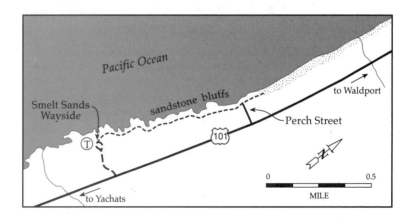

Off Yachats 804 Trail

From the center of Yachats, north of Florence, take US Highway 101 north 0.5 mile and turn west at the sign to Smelt Sands Wayside. The gravel road leads 0.3 mile to a parking area and signed trailhead.

Just past the trailhead there are picnic tables perched on the bluff and a small, sandy beach below. The wide, compacted-gravel path (wheelchair-accessible) heads north, following the edge of the bluff. A few steps down the trail look west to see a rock tunnel that becomes a wild blowhole at high tide. The rocks are great fun to explore at low tide, potentially hazardous at high tide.

Continuing north, the trail then leads into a stand of shore pines and skirts a narrow chasm at about 0.4 mile. Near the end it crosses Perch Street and drops down a sandstone bank to end at the beach at 0.75 mile. The beach stretches several miles to the north; follow it as far as you'd like and return as you came.

87 CAPE PERPETUA

Type ▪ Day hike
Hikable ▪ Year-round
Contact ▪ Cape Perpetua Scenic Area,
(541) 547-3289

SHORELINE LOOP

Difficulty ▪ Easy for children
Distance ▪ 1.3 miles, loop
Terrain ▪ Mostly level; slight ascent
High point ▪ 140 feet

GIANT SPRUCE TRAIL

Difficulty ▪ Easy for children
Distance ▪ 0.4 to 2 miles round trip
Terrain ▪ Nearly level
High point ▪ 200 feet

DISCOVERY LOOP

Difficulty ▪ Easy to moderate for children
Distance ▪ 2 miles round trip
Terrain ▪ Steady ascent (680 feet elevation gain)
High point ▪ 800 feet

From a sweet cove beach with blowholes and tide pools at either end to the steep, forested headland towering above, Cape Perpetua Scenic Area offers plenty of options to hikers of all ages and energy levels. These three are good starting points with children; check at the interpretive center here for information on longer hikes into the forest. Begin at the area's interpretive center, about 3 miles south of Yachats off US Highway 101.

SHORELINE LOOP

Link Captain Cook Trail with Restless Waters Trail for a 1.3-mile loop above the coastline. You could actually start at any of several pullouts along the highway and find your own way onto the loop. From the interpretive center, follow signs down a trail heading west, under the highway. At the end of the pedestrian tunnel, turn left and walk toward Spouting Horn, a hole in the top of a sea cave that spouts

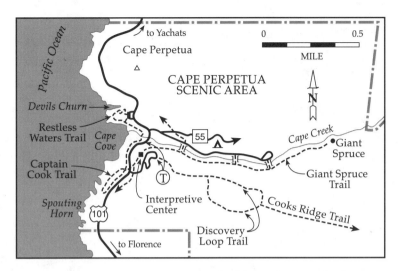

air and water when incoming waves build pressure inside the cave. Continue around to the south to do some tide pooling, if tide permits. Return to the junction to continue the loop. Along the way, notice the mounds on the bluff above the beach. They're Indian middens—essentially garbage dumps—used by the Alsi Indians between about A.D. 600 and 1620. Archeologists believe the Alsi camped here in the summer while collecting mussels and other shellfish to eat. They tossed the discarded shells in a heap, along with bones from fish, birds, and animals they caught.

From the tunnel, head north to reach Cape Cove Beach (look for a little spur trail leading to the beach on the south side of Cape Creek) and eventually Devils Churn. There you'll find a dead-end rock chute where waves race in and, at higher tide, crash dramatically, drenching visitors who stand too close. It was formed over thousands of years through the slow process of erosion; a crack in the basalt slab at the sea's edge was slowly worn into the chute you see today by the pounding of zillions of waves.

Spur trails loop back up to the highway at several spots, but you can follow the trail as far as curiosity leads, then return roughly as you came.

GIANT SPRUCE TRAIL

The destination on this short, level hike is a 500-year-old Sitka spruce that kids can crawl under, thanks apparently to its having sprouted on a nurse log that's long since decayed and disappeared.

Rocks at Devils Churn

The hike is ideal for preschoolers or for anyone looking for a short, leg-stretching outing along the coast. From the interpretive center, follow signs onto a paved path heading north toward Cape Creek. The path reaches a footbridge at 0.2 mile, but rather than crossing into the Cape Perpetua Campground, continue east another 0.6 mile along the musical creek's south bank to a footbridge at the end of the campground. (For an even shorter hike, drive to this point and start here.) From the footbridge it's a mostly level, 0.2 mile stretch to the giant spruce. The famed tree is about 15 feet in diameter and was 225 feet tall—until a 1962 windstorm snapped off its upper 35 feet.

DISCOVERY LOOP

For a short forest hike, head up Cooks Ridge Trail, which starts at the upper end of the parking lot above the interpretive center. The trail begins in dense Douglas fir and spruce and then leads into a lovely stand of old-growth Sitka spruce at about 0.7 mile, where a junction signals the start of a 0.6-mile midtrail loop. Hike the loop and return as you came for a 2-mile round trip. More energetic hikers could continue beyond the loop, which slowly ascends Cooks Ridge to link with other forest trails.

88 HOBBIT BEACH–CHINA CREEK

Type ■ Day hike
Hikable ■ Year-round
Contact ■ Carl G. Washburne State Park,
(541) 547-3416

HOBBIT BEACH
Difficulty ■ Easy for children
Distance ■ 0.5 mile round trip
Terrain ■ Gentle ascent on return (200 feet elevation gain)
High point ■ 200 feet

CHINA CREEK LOOP
Difficulty ■ Moderate for children
Distance ■ 3.4 miles, loop
Terrain: ■ Gradual ascent (120 feet elevation gain)
High point ■ 200 feet

What would a hobbit's trail look like? It would most likely be hidden, a little tunnel through deep woods, with fantastical, moss-covered trees. It might even be a little spooky, and it should definitely lead to a magical place. Certainly the Hobbit Trail fits that description. Take it to Hobbit Beach, or follow the China Creek Trail into the forest east of the highway for wonderful woods walking and picnicking along the shallow creek.

Both hikes start at a signed trailhead on the east side of US Highway 101 about 12 miles north of Florence (1.2 miles south of the entrance to Carl G. Washburne State Park, or 0.8 mile north of the entrance to Heceta Head Lighthouse State Scenic Viewpoint).

HOBBIT BEACH

The trail begins at a wooden trail post on the west side of the highway. Cars zoom by pretty fast here; watch kids carefully while lacing shoes and loading packs. From the trailhead go west, continuing straight at the junction (a left turn leads to Heceta Head Lighthouse, Hike 89). The path winds through a forest of pines and spruce and tall rhododendrons, twisting downhill 0.25 mile. It's easy to

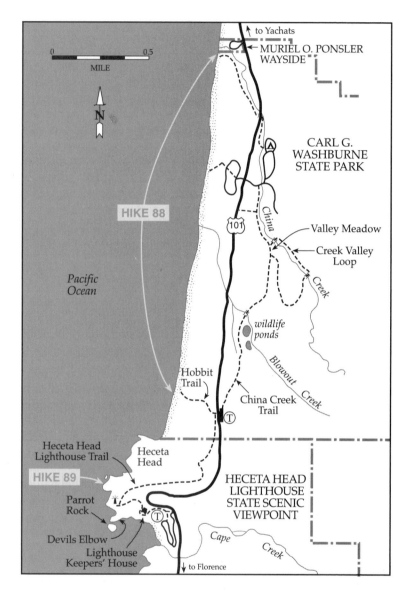

imagine running into a hobbit scurrying along this trail—or to imagine you are one yourself. Approaching the beach, the trail drops into a narrow sand chute, with salal closing in overhead. Suddenly you're on the beach just north of the massive Heceta Head. Return as you came, or link with China Creek Trail for a longer loop (see below).

CHINA CREEK LOOP

Often overlooked in favor of the Hobbit Trail, this trail winds through the gorgeous coastal forest on either side of China Creek, south of the campground at Carl G. Washburne State Park. From the trailhead shared with the Hobbit Trail, the trail drops down briefly, then levels off, following the route of the old coast highway north along slow-moving Blowout Creek. At 0.5 mile the trail passes a couple of ponds; look for evidence of beavers. It crosses a creek and then continues north through the woods. A few steps before the trail emerges from the trees and drops down into sunny Valley Meadow at 1.3 miles, you'll reach a spur trail to the right. Take it, crossing a small creek on a culvert. The trail heads up briefly, then zigzags south and east across a carpet of moss, to the accompaniment of the ocean's roar. It drops down and veers north, crossing a footbridge at babbling China Creek at 0.5 mile, then follows the creek's east bank to a second footbridge at Valley Meadow 0.75 mile after leaving the main trail. Return to the main trail and follow it south back to your starting point.

Hobbit Trail

For a longer loop hike, continue north from Valley Meadow on the main trail into the park's campground, picking up a trail to the beach at the campground's far end and following it to the beach. Walk the beach south to Hobbit Beach and return to your car via the Hobbit Trail (total loop: 4.75 miles). Shorten the loop to 3.75 miles by walking out the campground entrance road, crossing the highway, and accessing the beach via the highway rest area.

89 HECETA HEAD LIGHTHOUSE

Type ▪ Day hike
High point ▪ 600 feet
Hikable ▪ Year-round
Contact ▪ Carl G. Washburne State Park, (541) 547-3416

FROM THE SOUTH
Difficulty ▪ Easy for children
Distance ▪ 1 mile round trip
Terrain ▪ Steady ascent (200 feet elevation gain)

FROM THE NORTH
Difficulty ▪ Moderate for children
Distance ▪ 3 miles round trip
Terrain ▪ Steady ascent (400 feet elevation gain)

The park at Heceta Head Lighthouse is a great family beach destination: the small enclosed cove invites wading and is just wide enough for kites on a windy day. A trail leads up the headland 0.5 mile to the century-old lighthouse—just right for a short hike. For a bit more challenge, walk to the lighthouse from the Hobbit Beach trailhead. With a shuttle car you could hike both trails end to end.

 The southern access trail starts at Heceta Head Lighthouse State Scenic Viewpoint (formerly Devils Elbow State Park), about 11 miles north of Florence off US Highway 101. Drive another mile to reach the northern trailhead, shared with the Hobbit Trail.

FROM THE SOUTH
Start at the north end of the parking area at Heceta Head Lighthouse State Scenic Viewpoint and follow the trail past picnic tables

Lighthouse keeper's house, Heceta Head

and up the hill, following an old wagon road. At about 0.25 mile you pass the restored lighthouse-keeper's house (now operated as a bed and breakfast); a spur trail leads west to a viewpoint overlooking Parrot Rock (so named in the late 1800s for the tufted puffins—"sea parrots"—that have since abandoned the island). Continue on the main trail another 0.25 mile to reach the 1893 lighthouse itself and views west of birds, whales, and maybe fishing boats. Return as you came.

FROM THE NORTH

Park at the Hobbit Beach trailhead, cross the highway to the beach trail, and immediately head south at the junction. For a short distance the trail runs parallel to the highway, then veers away into a draw, and starts up the airy forested hillside, first on steps and then on a series of switchbacks. At 0.75 mile it levels off at a view of the coastline to the north, then drops down into a dark spruce forest, switchbacking before it meets the old lighthouse trail just east of the light. Return as you came.

90 KENTUCKY FALLS

Type ▪ Day hike
Difficulty ▪ Moderate for children
Distance ▪ 4 miles round trip
Terrain ▪ Steady ascent on return (760 feet elevation gain)
High point ▪ 1560 feet
Hikable ▪ Year-round
Contact ▪ Mapleton Ranger District, (541) 902-8526

It's necessary to drive a bit to get to the trailhead for Kentucky Falls, but it's worth it. The hike in is easy—almost too easy—and the mostly downhill trail ends at a pair of side-by-side waterfalls at the confluence of two creeks. Winter rains swell the falls, adding to their drama. Though the trail is snow-free virtually all year, snow sometimes blocks the road around 2862-foot Roman Nose Mountain; in winter, call the Mapleton Ranger District for road conditions.

 From State Highway 126 about 35 miles west of Eugene (between mileposts 26 and 27), turn south at the sign to Clay Creek and Whittaker Creek Recreation Site. Go 1.5 miles and turn right, then another 1.5 miles and bear left. In 6.9 miles turn left, following a sign to Reedsport. In 2.7 miles turn right onto Forest Road 23. Go 1.6

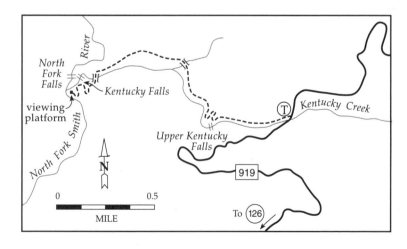

Kentucky Falls

miles, turn right on Forest Road 919 and continue 2.7 miles to the trailhead. All but 4.5 miles are paved. You can also drive here on forest roads from Reedsport, but it's a longer trip.

Follow the trail into gorgeous old-growth and second-growth forest, listening for bird songs and looking for wildflowers in spring. After about 0.6 mile of fairly level walking, you'll reach a viewpoint overlooking Upper Kentucky Falls. The trail then drops quickly to the falls' base.

The trail follows Kentucky Creek then winds away from it a short distance to cross a side creek on a railed log bridge at 1.4 miles. For the last 0.4 mile the trail switchbacks steadily into the canyon, signaling to children that they're nearing the end (and that they'd better steel themselves for the return hike).

At the trail's end, you will see both the North Fork Smith River and Kentucky Creek cascading down a cliff just upstream of the two creeks' confluence. A wooden viewing platform at the end covers a tangle of boulders that used to make viewing the falls a dangerous proposition for all but the most nimble-footed; now it's quite safe. Explore around the base of the falls a bit before turning around and tackling the return trip.

91 SWEET CREEK

Type ■	Day hike
Difficulty ■	Easy for children
Distance ■	3 miles one way
Terrain ■	Gradual ascent, with steep stretches (480 feet elevation gain)
High point ■	600 feet
Hikable ■	Year-round
Contact ■	Mapleton Ranger District, (541) 902-8526

Visit in winter, when the creek is full and the falls roar over bedrock ledges. Better yet, visit in midsummer to wade across those ledges, splash in shallow pools, and savor the sun and dappled shade of this very sweet creek. An elaborate trail reconstruction, including extensive boardwalks, adds to the fun of a kids' hike here. It's in the foothills of the Coast Range, about a half-hour from US Highway 101.

From the east end of the Siuslaw River Bridge in Mapleton (on State Highway 126, 14 miles east of Florence), turn south on Sweet Creek Road (County Road 48). Go 11 miles and look for the Homestead trailhead on the right.

You can access four trailheads from Sweet Creek Road. Most hikers start at the first one, the Homestead trailhead (the only one with a rest room). From here it's a bit more than 1 mile up the gorge by trail to one of the creek's main attractions, 90-foot Sweet Creek Falls.

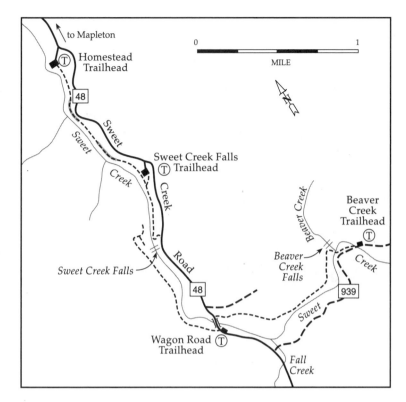

This trail section is especially appealing; where the creek gorge narrows, a railed catwalk hugs the cliff above the churning water. If this 1-mile trek is more hike than you want, drive 0.5 mile farther to the Sweet Creek Falls trailhead. The falls are just 0.5 mile by trail from here. Spur trails on either side of the creek lead to views of water splashing down the basalt staircase.

Although the trail seems to end at the falls, in fact it resumes across the boulder-strewn creek. There's no footbridge, and a midwinter crossing on slick rocks isn't recommended with children. Agile, older children can manage the crossing in summer; look for the trail heading up the opposite bank and follow it to where it meets the road at a road bridge. (Or drive 0.75 mile farther to Wagon Road trailhead, adjacent to the road bridge). From this third trailhead it's 0.5 mile by trail to Beaver Creek Falls, where the main trail ends. The fourth trailhead, Beaver Creek, lies off a signed spur road (Forest Road 939) just up Road 48 and leads down a separate, short trail to a view of Beaver Falls from above.

Sweet Creek

92 WAXMYRTLE TRAIL

Type	Day hike
Difficulty	Easy for children
Distance	2.5 miles round trip
Terrain	Nearly level
High point	40 feet
Hikable	Year-round
FYI	No dogs on Estuary Trail
Contact	Oregon Dunes National Recreation Area, (541) 271-3611

This trail follows the meandering Siltcoos River for its last 1.25 miles before reaching the ocean. It's short enough for almost any child to hike, and the ever-present opportunity to see wild birds on or near the river entertains kids as they walk. Changing views also keep things interesting along the way. At the end, there's the beach. Be sure to pack in a kite!

From Florence take US Highway 101 south about 7 miles and turn west onto Siltcoos Beach Road. Follow it 1 mile and park in the Stagecoach trailhead parking area on the left, just west of the entrance to Waxmyrtle Campground.

On foot, backtrack 0.1 mile on trail to the Waxmyrtle Campground road, cross the Siltcoos River, and turn west where the trail begins following the river's south bank. Climb stairs up a short hill forested with shore pines, continuing along the bluff. At 0.4 mile there's a junction. Bear right on the "Estuary Trail" and you'll follow a riverside route out to the beach (may be difficult at high tide). No dogs are allowed on this trail. This is a good stretch for seeing cormorants, kingfishers, great blue herons, and other water-loving birds. Otherwise, bear left on "Beach Access Trail" leading onto an old sand road; 0.4 mile from the junction you'll reach Waxmyrtle Marsh, on the left. The marsh is an old channel of the Siltcoos River that was cut off over time; water birds visit throughout the year, and beaver and nutria live here as well. Continue another 0.25 mile to the beach. Return as you came, or loop around to return on the Estuary Trail, if tide permits.

For more fun exploring: Back at the trailhead cross Siltcoos Beach Road to the start of 1-mile River of No Return loop trail, which follows an old arm of the Siltcoos River around Lagoon Campground on a combination of boardwalk and footpath.

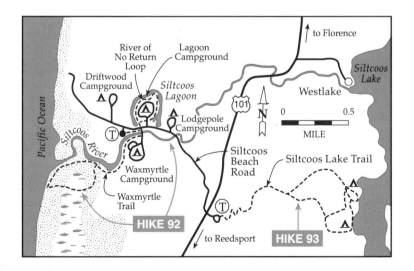

Nearing the beach on Waxmyrtle Trail

93 SILTCOOS LAKE

Type ▪	Day hike or backpack
Difficulty ▪	Moderate for children
Distance ▪	5 miles round trip
Terrain ▪	Level or gentle ascent (600 feet elevation gain)
High point ▪	380 feet
Hikable ▪	Year-round
Contact ▪	Oregon Dunes National Recreation Area, (541) 271-3611

Most hikes in Oregon Dunes National Recreation Area start or end at the beach. This one takes you east from the highway through deep forest to a big lake. It's not a wilderness hike—you can see homes along the lakeshore, and the lakeside campsites are accessible to motorboats as well. But the hike itself is a pleasant one, and the lake offers a refreshing reward to hot hikers in summer.

The trailhead is on the east side of US Highway 101 across from Siltcoos Beach Road, about 7 miles south of Florence. Begin hiking up a steady incline through dense shrubbery. The trail levels off and then at 1 mile splits into two trails. Either direction leads to the lake in a little more than 1 mile. On the left-hand trail, the route drops slowly through second-growth forest logged long ago (look for old-time loggers' springboard notches in stumps). At 2.2 miles a spur trail leads left to a group of five lakeside campsites; continue around the lakeshore to a single, lovely campsite to the south. (On our last visit there were outhouses at both campsites, but both were in very bad condition.) The campground loops are a bit confusing here, but bear left and you'll eventually wind around to the return trail. It leads over a boardwalk and up a set of stairs, then skirts the bottom of a clearcut 0.3 mile before completing the loop. Bear left to return to the trailhead.

Siltcoos Lake Trail

94 OREGON DUNES OVERLOOK

Type ■ Day hike

Hikable ■ Year-round

Contact ■ Oregon Dunes National Recreation Area, (541) 271-3611

BEACH

Difficulty ■ Easy for children

Distance ■ 2 miles round trip

Terrain ■ Nearly level after descent from overlook

High point ■ 140 feet

BEACH TRAIL LOOP

Difficulty ■ Moderate for children

Distance ■ 3.3 miles, loop

Terrain ■ Level or short ascents (300 feet elevation gain)

High point ■ 140 feet

The Oregon Dunes Overlook was built to give motorists a taste of the dunes on a quick detour off US Highway 101. It's also the trailhead for a wonderfully varied loop hike that takes in open dunes, the ocean beach, tree islands, and coastal forest. Though there's not much elevation gain, it's more difficult than forest hikes of comparable distance because much of the walking is on soft sand. Post-to-post routefinding across the shifting dunes adds an element of adventure.

BEACH

The overlook is off US 101 about 10 miles south of Florence (and about the same distance north of Reedsport). You can reach the main trail from one of two directions: either walk down a winding, sandy trail from the upper viewing deck, or follow the long switchbacks on the trail leading down the hill from the main covered viewing structure adjacent to the parking lot. Both approaches take you to the middle of an open dune; from here, posts mark the route west across about 0.3 mile of open sand. To reach the beach, bear right with the posts to enter the deflation plain, which the trail crosses with help from small bridges. Climbing over the foredune, the trail reaches the beach at 1 mile.

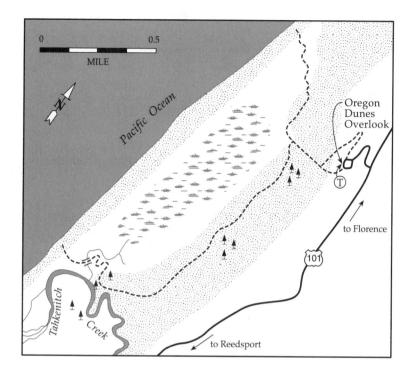

BEACH TRAIL LOOP

For a loop hike, walk south along the beach for 1.5 miles until you see a trail post in the foredune (if you reach Tahkenitch Creek, you've gone too far). The trail leads up and over the foredune, granting a glimpse of Tahkenitch Creek on the right; pause to look for ospreys and bald eagles. Cross a little footbridge 0.2 mile from the beach, then head up into a tall "island" of shore pines. From the summit you'll again see the creek. Drop down the other side of the tree island and begin trekking across a Sahara-like landscape of open dunes, following marker posts leading to another tree island. Follow the trail around the tree island's west side, then get back on the open sand. The trail skirts west of the next big tree island. (Look carefully for the post here; it's deeply buried in sand and hard to spot.) Just before reaching the end of the loop in the open sand below the overlook, the trail enters the deflation plain and becomes a narrow, sandy path.

For more fun exploring: Stop in at the Oregon Dunes visitors center just off US 101 in Reedsport for information on the dunes ecology and geology and more hiking suggestions.

Oregon Dunes Overlook loop trail

95 UMPQUA DUNES

Type ▪ Day hike
Hikable ▪ Year-round
Contact ▪ Oregon Dunes National Recreation Area, (541) 271-3611

INTERPRETIVE LOOP

Difficulty ▪ Easy for children
Distance ▪ 1 mile, loop
Terrain ▪ Short ascent (120 feet elevation gain)
High point ▪ 120 feet

BEACH TRAIL

Difficulty ▪ Strenuous for children
Distance ▪ 5 miles round trip
Terrain ▪ Ups and downs on soft sand (120-plus feet elevation gain)
High point ▪ 120 feet

The most adventurous and challenging of all the trails in Oregon Dunes National Recreation Area is the walk across Umpqua Dunes to the beach. It's perhaps too adventurous for many children; others

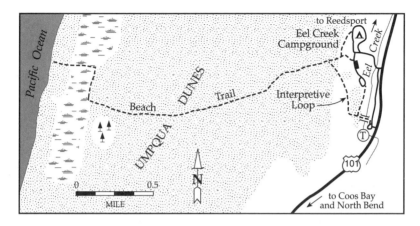

(older, more determined) will find it thrilling, certainly doable if you take it slow and pick a good weather day. It begins on an easy interpretive loop trail that any child could handle, with a spur to campsites at Eel Creek Campground. Then the loop trail ends and the real adventure begins: crossing the widest swath of open dunes in the entire Oregon dunes, with help from a few widely scattered wooden posts. Hikers need to stay on their toes and do a little common-sense orienteering to get back to where they started. The elevation figure listed with the hike is just the rise from the parking lot to the edge of the open dunes; you could easily quadruple that figure hiking up and down the open dunes on the way to the beach. This hike is no fun on a wet or windy day.

Umpqua Dunes

The signed trailhead parking area is 8 miles south of Reedsport or 12 miles north of North Bend off US Highway 101, just south of Eel Creek Campground. A long footbridge immediately crosses Eel Creek and leads to a junction, the start of the interpretive loop. Bear right or left; either way will lead you up and around to a tall dune at the edge of the open sand. Enjoy some climbing and sliding before completing the loop, if that's as much as you want to tackle.

To reach the beach, head west across the open dunes, keeping the big tree island on your left. Wooden posts are helpful but not really necessary. When you reach the end of the open sand at the edge of the vegetated deflation plain, turn north; signs will lead you to the start of a trail through the marsh to the beach. Most of the year this trail is very soggy; consider wearing waterproof sandals, because you're going to get wet. Cross the tall foredune and drop down to the beach. Return as you came. On the return trip across the open sand, aim toward the blue water tower in the distance to land in the general vicinity of the interpretive trail, which will lead you back to your car.

96 CAPE ARAGO

Type ▪	Day hike
Difficulty ▪	Moderate for children
Distance ▪	3.5 miles one way
Terrain ▪	Mostly level, with short ascents (120 feet elevation gain)
High point ▪	120 feet
Hikable ▪	Year-round
Contact ▪	Sunset Bay State Park, (541) 888-3778

Three contiguous state parks south of Charleston offer diverse opportunities to families, including swimming (or wading) in a protected cove, strolling through formal gardens, and picnicking on a bluff overlooking the Pacific. What most visitors to this area never see, however, is the dramatic, rocky shoreline that's only accessible by trail. So pull on some boots (it's muddy in places) and walk part or all of the Oregon Coast Trail between Sunset Bay Park, Shore Acres Park, and the viewpoint 0.5 mile north of Cape Arago. Hike as a one-way trek with a shuttle car, or consider a round-trip hike from, say, Sunset Bay to Shore Acres (3.6 miles).

Follow signs from Coos Bay or North Bend about 9 miles to Charleston, then continue south on Cape Arago Highway about 5 miles to Sunset Bay Park. The road continues about 3 miles, past Shore Acres State Park, to end at Cape Arago State Park.

Look for a trail post near the rest rooms at the south end of the Sunset Bay State Park parking area. Cross the footbridge over Big Creek, ascend the headland, and bear right around a big mowed meadow, then continue south along the bluff. At 0.6 mile the trail leads back out to the highway, follows it south a short distance, and resumes at a stile over the guardrail. It continues through woods some

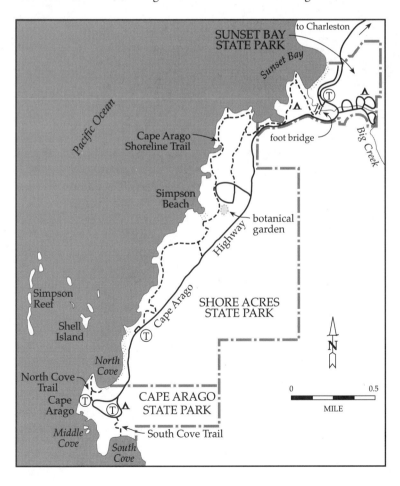

Shoreline between Sunset Bay and Shore Acres State Park

 distance from the shoreline; at a junction, veer north and west out to the bluff, where you'll view the lighthouse to the north and rocks to the south (or continue straight for a shortcut through the forest to Shore Acres State Park).

Approaching Shore Acres at about 1.8 miles, either detour east and enter the botanical gardens (exiting through the open gate at the back of the gardens, where you can pick up the trail again) or follow a trail winding to the west of the gardens. In either case, stick to the paved paths to avoid confusion. From Shore Acres the trail leads down to intimate Simpson Beach, into woods, and then back up onto a bluff. At the trail junction, bear right. (A left turn leads to the highway.) The trail leads out to the shore, back to the highway briefly at 3.3 miles, resumes as trail, and ends at a viewpoint overlooking Shell Island, 0.5 mile north of the road's end at Cape Arago State Park. Bring binoculars for the best views of the sea lions, harbor seals, and elephant seals seen on the island at various seasons.

For more exploring: From the Cape Arago State Park parking loop at the end of the highway, follow trails 0.2 mile down to the cape's north cove (closed March 1 through July 1) or south cove (open year-round) for tide pooling, wildlife watching, and beach playing.

97 SOUTH SLOUGH

Type ■ Day hike
Hikable ■ Year-round
Contact ■ South Slough National Estuarine Research
Reserve, (541) 888-5558

BIG CEDAR TRAIL
Difficulty ■ Easy for children
Distance ■ 1.5 miles round trip
Terrain ■ Nearly level
High point ■ Near sea level

HIDDEN CREEK TRAIL
Difficulty ■ Easy to moderate for children
Distance ■ 2.5 miles round trip
Terrain ■ Steady ascent from shore (180 feet
elevation gain)
High point ■ 180 feet

INTERPRETIVE CENTER TRAIL
Difficulty ■ Moderate for children
Distance ■ 3 miles round trip
Terrain ■ Steady ascent from shore (320 feet
elevation gain)
High point ■ 320 feet

The South Slough of Coos Bay was designated a national estuarine reserve in 1974 to preserve this relatively complete estuarine system for study and recreation. Three trails lead to a two-level viewing platform alongside the estuary, and from there to what's called Sloughside Pilings, where old dikes are slowly being reclaimed by the tides. Among those three trails, Big Cedar Trail is the shortest and easiest, built to accommodate wheelchairs; disabled visitors may stop at the interpretive center and pick up a key to the locked gate on the access road (call ahead). Hidden Creek is the most popular; it follows the tripping creek to a boardwalk through a skunk cabbage bog. The trail from the interpretive center is the longest and steepest. Begin your visit with a stop at the interpretive center, if it's open, where displays geared for children help orient youngsters for what they'll see on the hike.

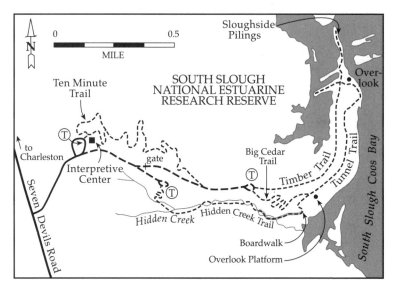

From US Highway 101 in North Bend or Coos Bay, follow signs about 8 miles southwest to Charleston. Turn left at the sign to South Slough and follow Seven Devils Road south 4.3 miles to the signed entrance to the research reserve, on the left. Trails start at the interpretive center (straight ahead), at the Hidden Creek trailhead (down a 0.2-mile spur road to the right), and the Big Cedar trailhead (access road is left off the Hidden Creek trailhead spur road; walk the 0.2 mile down the road or, with a key to the gate, drive).

BIG CEDAR TRAIL

Two trails start at the trailhead; take the right-hand trail and follow a gently descending route on gravel path and curving wooden boardwalk 0.25 mile to the viewing platform.

HIDDEN CREEK TRAIL

From the hidden creek trailhead, drop down the hillside, crossing and recrossing Hidden Creek as it flows to the slough. At sea level, a long, wooden boardwalk leads through a skunk cabbage bog, odorous and bright yellow in early spring, even in late winter. The route skirts a corner of the salt marsh and then makes a brief zigzag ascent to the viewing platform.

INTERPRETIVE CENTER TRAIL

Begin hiking the Ten-Minute Trail, but leave the loop and follow the trail down the hill. At 0.4 mile the trail reaches gravel Big Cedar

Trail access road; cross it to pick up Hidden Creek Trail or follow the road down 0.1 mile to pick up the Big Cedar Trail to the viewing platform.

From the viewing platform you can follow the Tunnel Trail to Sloughside Pilings (0.5 mile). The Tunnel Trail leads through dense forest, passes another overlook, and heads down steps approaching the edge of the water. Spur trails lead out along the marsh and onto old dikes. The dikes were built years ago by homesteaders reclaiming the marsh for pasture land. Now they're slowly crumbling, as the estuary returns to its natural state. Return to the viewing platform as you came, or take the Timber Trail—part footpath, part sand road—that gently winds back to the Big Cedar trailhead.

For more fun exploring: Ask at the interpretive center about the short loop trails at Wasson and Winchester Creeks, south of main trail system.

Boardwalk along South Slough

98 HUMBUG MOUNTAIN

Type ■ Day hike
Difficulty ■ Strenuous for children
Distance ■ 5 to 6 miles round trip
Terrain ■ Steady ascent (1730 feet elevation gain)
High point ■ 1730 feet
Hikable ■ Year-round
Contact ■ Humbug Mountain State Park,
(541) 332-6774

Taxing enough for adults, I wouldn't have thought to recommend this hike for children—if I hadn't shared the summit views with a pair of youngsters who had beat me to the top. Forested Humbug Mountain dominates the south coast with its steep rise from tide pools to sky. In spring, wildflowers brighten the trail side and the creeks are raucous. In autumn, fallen bay leaves crunch underfoot, sending their spicy fragrance into the air. There isn't a season when the hike up Humbug Mountain isn't appealing.

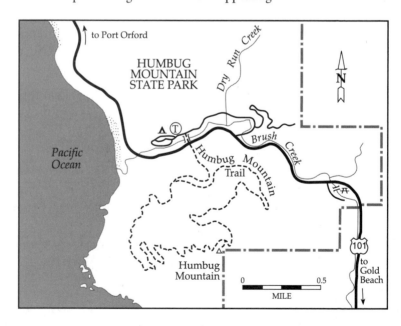

View north from Humbug Mountain

The trailhead for the summit ascent is on the north side of US Highway 101 just west of the entrance to Humbug Mountain State Park campground, about 6 miles south of Port Orford. (Another access trail from the campground leads across Brush Creek and under the highway.) The trail immediately crosses a small creek and begins climbing through an airy forest of Douglas fir, rhododendrons, and bay trees; it continues up at a moderately steep grade.

Just past a 1-mile marker the trail splits. Bear left and it's another 2 miles to the summit; bear right and it's 1.5 miles to the same point. The 1.5-mile route reopened in 1993, twenty-five years after it was closed following a major blowdown of trees during the Northwest's infamous Columbus Day storm. Enjoy the views of the ocean and Port Orford on this stretch of trail. Just short of the summit the two approaches meet; follow the trail a few paces to the summit, where you can drink in the view to the south from a small, grassy clearing. Return as you came or loop back to the junction on the alternate trail.

99 INDIAN SANDS

Type ■ Day hike
Difficulty ■ Easy for children
Distance ■ 0.4 mile to 5 miles round trip
Terrain ■ Rolling (150 to 350 feet elevation gain)
Hikable ■ Year-round
High point ■ 350 feet
Contact ■ Harris Beach State Park, (541) 469-2021

Boardman State Park is a great resource for hiking families. The narrow park is stretched out along the coastline between Pistol River and Brookings and is threaded by the Oregon Coast Trail, running between the ocean and US Highway 101. Many trailheads are scattered along the highway, dividing the trail into sections ranging from about 0.5 mile to 3 miles. If willing to take a chance, just pull over at one of the signed viewpoints or trailhead parking areas and start walking; you really can't lose. Fall is a particularly nice time to hike here, as weather tends to be good and the trail not too brushy (it's rather overgrown in spring before trail crews arrive). Watch for poison oak, especially on the trail between Whalehead Beach and Indian Sands.

One of the most interesting sections is known as Indian Sands, at about the middle of the park. For quick access to this area of

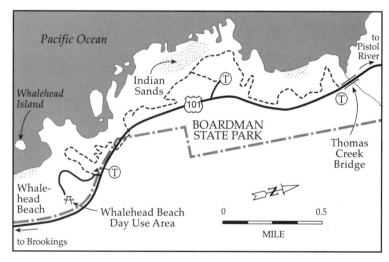

Boardman State Park

sculptured cliffs, arches, and coves, pull into the Indian Sands parking area off US Highway 101 just south of milepost 348 (about 12 miles north of Brookings) and follow the trail 0.2 mile down through coastal forest to the shore. Emerging from the trees you'll find yourself in a fantasy land where wind and water have sculpted the open dunes and ochre sandstone into marvelous shapes.

For a longer hike, include Indian Sands in a 2.5-mile hike from Thomas Creek Bridge south to Whalehead Beach, or make a 1.7-mile hike from Indian Sands to Whalehead Beach. A shuttle car provides the option of one-way hikes. The northern trailhead, off the parking area at the south end of Thomas Creek Bridge, is south of milepost 347 off US 101. The southern trailhead is at the top of the road leading off US 101 to Whalehead Beach, south of milepost 349.

From Thomas Creek Bridge, follow the trail down a draw, through a forest of Sitka spruce, and across an open hillside. The trail swings back to US 101 at 0.5 mile. Walk along the highway a short distance, then pick up the trail again, following it down a steep draw. It's more dramatic than hazardous in here, but keep an eye on children. Turn a corner, climb over a saddle, and follow posts through the sand a short distance to Indian Sands, at about 1 mile.

Continue south, following the posts, to where the trail resumes, leading into shady woods. It crosses a couple of creeks, then leads out to the highway 0.8 mile from Indian Sands. Walk south inside the guardrail about 40 yards until the trail resumes in a salal-bordered corridor leading into a forest of Sitka spruce. The trail climbs a bit, then offers a peek into a hidden cove. Round a corner to get a grand view of Whalehead Beach, then switchback down to the parking area at the top of the road to Whalehead.

For more fun exploring: Whalehead Beach is the longest (1.5 miles) beach in Boardman State Park. With rest rooms and picnic tables, it makes a good base camp for a day of south coast hiking.

100 REDWOOD NATURE TRAIL

Type ■ Day hike
Difficulty ■ Easy to moderate for children
Distance ■ 1 to 2.5 miles, loop
Terrain ■ Steady ascent (370 feet elevation gain)
High point ■ 470 feet
Hikable ■ Year-round
Contact ■ Harris Beach State Park, (541) 469-2021

There's something special about being in a redwood forest. The big trees with their reddish bark and lacy-needle boughs draping loftily overhead create a magical atmosphere. This trail is all the more fun because it's unexpected. First, redwoods are supposed to be in California, not Oregon. (These are actually the northernmost redwoods in the world.) Second, the lushness of the forest here, a few miles

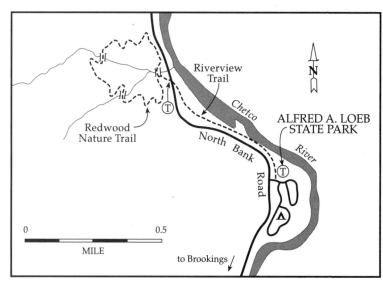

Redwood Nature Trail

inland, contrasts sharply with the often-open headlands of the south coast for those traveling along US Highway 101. The hike is short, but there are some fairly steep stretches, making it feel more like a real hike than just a nature walk.

In Brookings, just north of the Chetco River Bridge on US 101, turn east onto North Bank Road. The 1-mile loop hike begins 8.4 miles up the road at a trailhead on the left. Pick up an interpretive pamphlet, if available, at the station by the rest room just up the trail. Shortly the trail reaches a junction; turn left to hike clockwise, following the order of numbered posts, which correspond with explanations in the trail pamphlet. The brochure focuses mostly on natural history but weaves in some human history as well; one post marks an old log-cage bear trap built years ago and long abandoned.

For the first 0.5 mile, Douglas firs predominate along the trail as it ascends steadily. After crossing a footbridge over a creek, you'll start seeing big redwoods and a lot of rhododendrons. The trail peaks at about 0.75 mile. Cross the creek again, then start switchbacking down through the forest to recross the creek and meet the start of the loop.

Extend the hike by starting at Alfred A. Loeb State Park, 0.6 mile east of the trailhead. The 0.75-mile Riverview Trail begins in the park's picnic area, on the left side of the park entrance road. The trail mostly rolls along, in and out of leafy ravines, threading a narrow corridor between the Chetco River and the road. With wide gravel bars and a lazy current, the river is inviting in summer and easy to access from the trail, especially toward either end. It ends across the road from Redwood Nature Trail.

INDEX

ABOUT THE AUTHOR

Bonnie Henderson grew up in Portland, Oregon, and spent most family vacations hiking and backpacking in Mount Hood National Forest. During college she began guiding whitewater raft trips and leading teenagers on wilderness backpacking trips in the Rocky, Cascade, and Olympic mountains, and later taught cross-country skiing at Mount St. Helens. She has a master's degree in journalism and spent six years as a travel writer with *Sunset* magazine. She is now a writer and editor and lives in Eugene, Oregon.

THE MOUNTAINEERS, founded in 1906, is a nonprofit outdoor activity and conservation club, whose mission is "to explore, study, preserve, and enjoy the natural beauty of the outdoors. . . ." Based in Seattle, Washington, the club is now the third-largest such organization in the United States, with 15,000 members and five branches throughout Washington State.

The Mountaineers sponsors both classes and year-round outdoor activities in the Pacific Northwest, which include hiking, mountain climbing, ski-touring, snowshoeing, bicycling, camping, kayaking and canoeing, nature study, sailing, and adventure travel. The club's conservation division supports environmental causes through educational activities, sponsoring legislation, and presenting informational programs. All club activities are led by skilled, experienced volunteers, who are dedicated to promoting safe and responsible enjoyment and preservation of the outdoors.

If you would like to participate in these organized outdoor activities or the club's programs, consider a membership in The Mountaineers. For information and an application, write or call The Mountaineers, Club Headquarters, 300 Third Avenue West, Seattle, Washington 98119; (206) 284-6310.

The Mountaineers Books, an active, nonprofit publishing program of the club, produces guidebooks, instructional texts, historical works, natural history guides, and works on environmental conservation. All books produced by The Mountaineers are aimed at fulfilling the club's mission.

Send or call for our catalog of more than 300 outdoor titles.

The Mountaineers Books
1001 SW Klickitat Way, Suite 201
Seattle, WA 98134
800-553-4453
mbooks@mountaineers.org
www.mountaineersbooks.org